SHE OUTWITTED THE MANDARINS

Famous Mysteries

CURIOUS AND FANTASTIC RIDDLES
OF HUMAN LIFE THAT HAVE
NEVER BEEN SOLVED

BY

JOHN ELFRETH WATKINS

PHILADELPHIA
THE JOHN C. WINSTON COMPANY
PUBLISHERS

CONTENTS

(5)

Contents

Contents 7

LIST OF ILLUSTRATIONS

FAMOUS MYSTERIES

CHAPTER I

Blood Royal or Common Clay?

Richard IV—Who Was He?

NEARLY every one is familiar with the picture of the two princes in the Tower of London—those sons of Edward IV alleged to have been murdered by order of their uncle, the Duke of Gloucester, who constituted himself King Richard III.

Indeed, for cold-blooded cruelty Richard III ranks in history with Nero, Torquemada and Ivan the Terrible. But destiny avenged herself upon him when Henry, Earl of Richmond, upturned his throne and constituted himself King Henry VII.

It was shortly after this, at the time of Columbus' discovery of America, that there appeared in Cork, Ireland, a mysterious personage who so strongly resembled the late King Edward IV, father of the princes in the tower, that he was immediately hailed as that monarch's brother,

(9)

the Duke of Clarence, supposed to have been murdered some years before. But this man of mystery took oath before the Mayor of Cork that he was not the Duke, whereupon the populace, still insisting that he was of royal blood, hailed him as a natural son of Richard III. This allegation being promptly denied by the newcomer, it was next averred that he was the son of the Duke of York, the younger of the two princes in the tower aforementioned. It then being estimated by men who knew their dates that the little Duke of York could not have left a son of that age, it was decided that the stranger was the Duke of York himself, which, after some hesitation, he admitted. According to his story, obtained from him with some difficulty, his elder brother, the young Prince of Wales, confined in the tower with him, had been assassinated just as history alleged, but on account of his youth his own life had been spared and he had been smuggled abroad, later escaping back to the British Isles, where he had lived in fear that his identity would be learned and that he would be slain by his enemies. Thus he acknowledged himself to be Richard Plantagenet, Duke of York, and, by right of succession, King Richard IV of England.

The people of Ireland flocked to his standard.

Many great nobles, coming from England, subjected him to rigid cross-questionings and went back to London convinced of the truth of his allegations. News of the identification reached the ears of Charles VIII of France who, being a bitter enemy of Henry VII of England, invited the young pretender to Paris, where he was received with royal honors. Shortly afterward Henry VII besieged Bologne and got the French King in such a tight place that he had to agree to a treaty banishing the alleged Richard IV. So that young man next went to Scotland, where King James IV fell on his neck and had him duly married to his relative, Catharine Gordon, daughter of the Earl of Huntly, who was to survive him and later marry three other husbands. But Henry of England forced the pretender out of Scotland and he turned against that monarch, invading England at the head of an army of Scotch soldiers. Repulsed, he next entered Cornwall and, leading 7,000 Cornishmen, marched upon London, suffering another defeat. He escaped to a monastery, but, being promised a pardon if he would surrender, delivered himself into the hands of Henry VII, who ('tis said, by torture) exacted from him an alleged confession that he was not the Duke of York, but one Perkin Warbeck, son of the Controller of Tournay, in Picardy, and that after an

adventurous career in Antwerp, Portugal and
other countries he had entered the service of one
Peter Vacz de Cogna, a one-eyed knight who had
shown him the world.   This alleged confession
was, of course, circulated widely by the King's
partisans, but there were some authorities familiar
with the Duke of York and the royal family who
stoutly maintained that the pretender was either
the younger prince of the tower or some other
member of the House of York.   Indeed, the
Duke of York's aunt, the Dowager Duchess of
Burgundy, Edward IV's own sister, hearing the
story of this man of mystery with distrust, sent
for him, and, after subjecting him to a rigid cross-
questioning, threw herself into his arms and
accepted him as her "beloved nephew Richard."
He was identified also by Sir Robert Clifford, who
had been well acquainted with the Duke of York,
and among hundreds of others who have accepted
his story were the famous historian, Thomas
Corte, and Horace Walpole, the great statesman
and scholar who became Earl of Oxford.   All who
saw the pretender agreed that he bore a wonderful likeness to his alleged father, Edward IV,
and that his manner measured up to princely
standards.   According to Lord Bacon, he readily
recognized the different members of the royal
family when he first arrived in England.   Some

modern authorities, including Stoker, believe that
he was the natural son of Edward IV. Indeed, it
has been discovered that the Warbeck who was
claimed in the alleged confession of the pretender as his father was a converted Jew, a god-
son of Henry IV, which monarch had been very
attentive to his wife.

After his supposed confession had been published, the alleged Richard IV was denied the
liberty guaranteed him. He was ignominiously
locked up in prison and subjected to various
humiliations, including commitment to the stocks,
whereupon he was forced to read his confession
aloud to the jeering multitude. And finally, eight
years after his advent in Cork, he was taken out
of jail and hanged.

Whether he was a rank impostor, a royal
victim of the bar sinister or the rightful Richard IV
will never be known. He is doomed to languish
among the enigmas of the centuries past.

The Mystery of Demetrius

Ivan the Terrible, the first ruler of Russia to
assume the title of Czar, yielded up his black soul
in 1584. His elder son and successor, Feodor, was
feeble-minded, and the next heir to the throne
was his younger son, Demetrius, a baby of two
years. So the people of Russia all centered their

hopes in this child who one day was to deliver them from the yoke held about their necks by an idiot. But Boris Godunoff, the Prime Minister, disposed of Feodor and proclaimed himself Czar of Russia. Old Ivan's widow, the empress dowager, was imprisoned in a convent and young Demetrius was kept under guard in the town of Uglich.

When Demetrius was a lad of nine all of his attendants were one day withdrawn and he was left alone to play in the courtyard. Suddenly a servant returning to the scene uttered a shriek of terror, and those who responded to her alarm found lying before them upon the ground a little boy with his throat cut from ear to ear, his features mutilated beyond recognition. The word was sent abroad through the empire that the sturdy little prince—the hope of the Russian populace—had been mysteriously murdered. There was universal mourning among the masses, but Boris Godunoff managed to retain his scepter for the time being.

In those days there dwelt in Poland a great prince, Adam Wisniowecki. He had a young servant who, fifteen years after the murder of the child at Uglich, fell ill, and fearing death confessed to a Jesuit priest that he was none other than the rightful Czar Demetrius, alleged to have been the victim of that crime. According to this youth's story, the agent whom Boris Godunoff had sent to Uglich had smuggled him off to Poland after mutilating a peasant lad resembling him in a general way and leaving that child's body in the courtyard to deceive the populace. In Poland he had been reared as a peasant, but his memory of his identity had not been outgrown. He repeated his confession to Wisniowecki and exhibited to that prince a diamond cross that had been the baptismal gift of little Demetrius, also a jeweled seal bearing the crest of that royal child.

Believing his servant's story, Wisniowecki lost no time in repeating it to Sigismund, the King of Poland, and, since that·monarch was a bitter enemy of Russia, he laid plans to upset the throne of Boris by furthering the claims of the mysterious youth claiming to be the rightful Czar. So Sigismund equipped a Polish army, and, placing the young pretender at the head of it, sent him into Russia in 1604. Demetrius was hailed with delight by some of the Russian populace, who hated the tyrannical usurper, Boris. They rallied to the young invader's standard and victory seemed to be within his grasp when, in a great battle on the plain of Dobrinichi, he suffered a serious defeat. In little more than a week later, however, Boris fell dead from poison and the alleged Demetrius led his army triumphant into the old capital of Moscow, where he demanded the crown.

The nobles at Moscow were more skeptical than had been the peasants outside. They hated Poland, and the story got abroad that the pretender was the tool of King Sigismund. They proposed that as a test of the young man's claim the mother of Demetrius be brought from her convent prison and asked to state whether the claimant to the throne was her son. So the widow of Ivan the Terrible was produced. Alone, in an inclosed tent, she received the pretender. They were together a long time. Then she emerged and announced to her one-time subjects that the young man was indeed her supposedly murdered son. She identified him beyond the shadow of a doubt. So he was crowned Czar of all the Russias in June, 1605.

At first Demetrius pleased his subjects with his wise and just policies, but hatred of Poland soon inflamed the Russians against him. They resented his introduction of Polish customs and his leaning toward the Polish religion. His people were naturally ambitious for him to marry a Russian princess, but his peasant rearing had given him fixed ideas of his own regarding affairs of the heart. Before his invasion of Russia he had become betrothed to Maryna Mniszek, a Polish girl of noble family, and within the year following his coronation he married her.   This infuriated the Russian aristocrats, who surrounded his palace May 29, 1605, the eleventh night after his wedding, and secretly broke into the bridal chamber.   Leaping from the window to the courtyard, thirty feet below, he broke his leg, and, being unable to reach his soldiers, succumbed to the assassins.   The leader of the band of murderers, Vasili Shuiski, seized the throne and threatened to torture old Ivan's widow.   In terror she admitted that the young man, who for nearly a year had ruled over Russia, was not her son, but that she had identified him in the hope of freeing herself from her convent prison and of enjoying a fortune which he had granted her.

In the minds of many Russians there is still a question whether this one-time servant of Prince Wisniowecki was indeed the rightful Czar or the impostor which his enemies purported him to be.

Who Was the Chevalier St. George?

When Charles II of England died without issue, his brother, the Duke of York, succeeded him in 1685 as James II, but immediately became unpopular by favoring the Church of Rome in violation of the act excluding Catholics from the throne.

So his eldest child, Mary, a Protestant, and her husband, William of Orange, were asked to cross the channel and "rescue the laws and religion of England."

During the previous year, 1688, it had been proclaimed that King James' consort was about to present him with a son, but for some reason there was spread abroad in the realm suspicion that her majesty was about to palm off upon the kingdom a supposititious child. It was a time when all kinds of rumors were rife. According to one of these, the Jesuits, by some feat of sleight-of-hand, were about to perpetrate the anticipated fraud. At last a child was produced, but those whose names were announced as witnesses to the birth did not command the public confidence.

"Some persons who were peculiarly entitled to be present and whose testimony would have satisfied all minds accessible to reason were absent," says Macaulay. Thus Protestant England imputed to the King and Queen the crime of foisting upon the realm, as heir to the throne, a male child not their own—that hapless little Prince, James Francis Edward Stuart, known later as the Chevalier St. George.

It was soon after the birth of this little Prince of Wales, who James II had hoped to be his successor, that the King had to flee to France, where, at the court of St. Germain, he gathered about him his Jacobite followers.

During those troublous times there dwelt in England Sir Theophilus Oglethorpe, a brave soldier who had been brigadier-general and and principal equerry to James II, and who, after the latter's flight, refused to serve against him. This refusal caused a warrant to be issued against Oglethorpe on the ground that he was a Jacobite, and he, too, escaped to France, although later returning to take the oath of allegiance to King William and to sit in Parliament.

Among Oglethorpe's various children were two daughters, Anne and Eleanor, who, during the family's exile in France, were reared as Catholics and who befriended the exiled King. On account of their religion and allegiance they could return to England only upon penalty of arrest.

After the return of Sir Theophilus to England, there came to his house to help with the sewing a young gentlewoman, Frances Shaftoe, who had come of good Northumberland stock. Two young women who shared the sewing with her were presented to her as "friends of Lady Oglethorpe" and the fact that their identities were cloaked in considerable mystery aroused her suspicions. At length she discovered that they were none others than Anne and Eleanor Oglethorpe, who had been smuggled over from France and were now hiding in their father's house that he might escape the penalty for harboring Catholics. After a time Frances Shaftoe, according to her later revelations, overheard these young women state that the infant Prince James, whose title to the throne had been so greatly doubted at the time of his alleged birth, had died at Windsor of convulsions and that Lady Oglethorpe had at the time hurried to town with her own little son, James, who, being only nine days older than the Prince of Wales, was substituted for him. The truth had remained a secret between Lady Oglethorpe and the Queen and all that the Oglethorpe girls knew at the time was that their infant brother had never again been seen.

Realizing that Frances Shaftoe shared the family secret, the Misses Oglethorpe took her to France, ostensibly on a pleasure trip and there shut her up in a convent where they thought it would be impossible for her to reveal the fact that "James Stuart" was really their brother, James Oglethorpe. But, after five years of imprisonment, Frances managed to smuggle to her mother a letter stating that she was being made a nun against her will and was suffering various indignities.

As a result, Anne Oglethorpe was arrested and

imprisoned, but, "having great allies," was discharged. At the time of Anne's hearing in court Frances Shaftoe's revelations were printed in a pamphlet which had great political effect in England. Shortly afterward Chevalier St. George, whose chances in Scotland had theretofore been most promising, failed in his attempts to regain his rights.

In later years, Westbrook Place, the Oglethorpe seat, is said to have harbored the Chevalier's son, "Bonnie Prince Charlie," the Young Pretender, and it was whispered that the old house had a secret vault where that prince could take refuge in case of a search. What truth there was in the various rumors purposed to repudiate the Chevalier St. George will, in all probability, never be known.

The Mystery of Stephen the Little

Catharine, daughter of the Prince Anhalt-Zerbst, married in 1745 Carl Peter Ulrich, grandson of Peter the Great. Seventeen years later, when her husband succeeded to the Russian throne as Czar Peter III she immediately entered into a conspiracy with her paramour, Gregory Orloff, to have him deposed. So Peter III was put in prison by his treacherous wife, who, six months after his succession, usurped his throne as

Catharine II.   She proved to be a strong ruler. No sovereign since Ivan the Terrible had extended the frontiers of the empire by such vast conquests as those effected by her armies.

After her husband was cast into prison it was given out that he had been put to death.   Five years later, however, a stranger appearing in Cattaro, a seaport of Dalmatia, was identified as the supposedly dead Peter III by a person who had once made a visit of state to the court of Russia.   According to this witness, the new-comer had the exact features and mannerisms of the late Czar, whom he had seen in St. Petersburg.

About this time there reigned over Montenegro the Vladika Sava, who, having been shut up for a score of years in a monastery, was not proving himself a strong ruler, such as was then needed to fight off the threatening Turks.   Montenegro was in a sore plight when there crossed its frontier no less a personage than the stranger previously identified at Cattaro as the lost Czar.   The story of his identity spread, and the man of mystery, with apparent reluctance, confessed that he really was Peter III.   As the Montenegrins were yearning for a strong ruler they listened to this stranger's story.   He related many wonderful adventures befalling him since his escape from the death intended for him by his false consort, and he stated that his disgust for his treacherous court was such that he would never return to Russia. So the Montenegrins lost no time in asking the newcomer to lead them against their enemies and the Vladika agreed to look after only the spiritual wants of his people if the supposed Czar would attend to their temporal affairs. Inasmuch as the Vladika combined the powers of pope and king, it was not such a difficult matter for him to divide his authority.

Thus "Stephen," as the alleged Peter III now became known, took over the actual government of Montenegro. He proved to be a strong ruler. Evil-doers were no longer able to escape punishment by bribery or threats. He established courts of law whose sentences were carried out. Thieves were shot and criminals of all classes began to tremble in their boots. He sought to improve transportation systems and went so far as to abolish Sunday labor.

Other nations appeared to have at first accepted Stephen's story of his identity, but gradually, as Montenegro's strength began to excite the anxiety of its neighbors, his pedigree was looked into more closely. Venice, becoming fearful that he would take Dalmatia away from her, joined with the Turks in a war against Montenegro. Although Stephen is said to have been terrified by the

approaching Turks, his courageous people fought
on against overwhelming odds, and just as
ignominious defeat was staring them in the face
their courage was rewarded by a strange stroke of
fate. There arose above the horizon a terrible
storm which broke just above the Turkish camp
and leveled it to the ground. While the Turks
fled in panic, the Montenegrins swooped down
upon their stores and seized a wealth of ammuni-
tion which enabled them to defeat their foes.

Montenegro now loomed up as a power to be
reckoned with. The Empress Catharine of Russia,
hitherto ignoring Stephen's claim to be her husband, began coquetting with the Montenegrins
by sending them war munitions, but at the same
time wrote a letter denouncing Stephen as an
impostor. As a result of her denunciation he
was put in prison and it was announced that he
admitted Catharine's accusation. If so his
alleged confession did not seem to spoil his people's
confidence in him. They demanded that his
strength be again enlisted for their protection.

Catharine then sent to Montenegro Prince
George Dolgourouki, who in her name made a
move which, in view of her supposed murder of her
husband and of Stephen's claim to being that
victim of her treachery, was indeed remarkable.
Taking Stephen out of prison, Dolgourouki

recognized him as regent and restored him to power under the auspices of Russia.

Thereafter "Stephen the Little," as he was known, successfully governed Montenegro until 1774, when, by order of his enemy, the Pasha of Scutari, he was assassinated by the Greek actor, Casamigna.

If Stephen the Little was an impostor, he was the only one in history who died upon a throne freely given to him.   Whoever he was, he possessed a high order of intellect, as well as wonderful resource.   According to the Vladika Sava, he was not in fact Peter III, but a descendant of Stefano Czernovich, the successor of Giorgio IV.

Who he really was is one of the great riddles of history.

The Identity of Louis Philippe

One of the arch villains of the French reign of terror was Louis, Duc d'Orleans, a direct descendant of King Louis XIII.   To save his neck during the revolution, he carried water on both shoulders.   Affecting sympathy with the people's cause, he renounced his titles, assumed the name of "Philippe Egalite" (Equality) and voted for the death of the unhappy Louis XVI, his kinsman.

But all of this while he was paving his way to

escape the guillotine, and, after the revolution should blow over, to secure succession to the throne for his own blood. He had taken to wife a royal princess, a kinswoman of his cousin the king, and his ambitions to have a son caused him great anxiety, for, according to the French law, no woman could succeed to the throne. So "Philip Equality" became the object of warm congratulation when it was announced that his first born was a boy, especially inasmuch as Louis XVI was at that time childless.

This lad in whom the cidevant Duc d'Orleans centered all his hopes was named Louis Philippe. But Philippe Egalite's schemes did not save his own villainous head. After the accession of the Jacobeans to power in the Convention and within less than a year after the execution of his cousin, Louis XVI, Philippe was, himself, carried to the dreadful guillotine. A year and a half later the little Dauphin of France mysteriously disappeared.* Then young Louis Philippe became involved in a conspiracy against the republic and was banished from France. His estate having been confiscated, he now found himself penniless and alone. After teaching school for a season in Switzerland, he traveled incognito through northern Europe and, declaring himself a Danish sub-

* See page 84.

ject, took passage on board a ship bound for
America.   Landing in Philadelphia, he was met
by his two exiled brothers and the three princes
traveled through New England, explored the
Great Lakes, toured the valley of the Mississippi,
saw the future site of the national capital and
visited General Washington at Mount Vernon.
Not until after he had been an exile from his
beloved France for more than twenty years did
there come the final overthrow of Napoleon and
the restoration of the Bourbon dynasty under
Louis XVIII.

Louis Philippe was now allowed to return home,
but his travels in the Land of the Free had intensi-
fied those liberal and democratic ideals which—
unlike Philippe Egalite—he cherished with honesty
and sincerity.   His espousal of these principles
soon offended Louis XVIII.   But that monarch's
rule was shortly to end and next came the succession of Charles X, whose policies, dictated by the
Church, precipitated the three days' revolution of
1830 and lost him the throne.   Philippe Egalite's
most cherished wish was now to be fulfilled.   The
crown was given to Louis Philippe as the result
of an election by the deputies and peers swayed
by the strong influence of Lafayette.

Because of his espousal of the plain people, the
new monarch was hailed "The Citizen King" and

he added to his popularity by calling himself
"King of the French" rather than "King of
France." But like all popular idols, his days of
influence were numbered. The populace grew
weary of him. After he had reigned for eighteen
years another revolution broke forth and his
throne was overturned. Disguising himself as a
scullion, he crept down the servants' stairway of
his palace and, taking his queen with him, escaped
to England, where he died two years later.

Although official history states that King Louis
Philippe was the son of Philippe Egalite, there
were persistent traditions that he was of very
humble birth. So far as Philippe Egalite was
concerned, his private life had been quite as
treacherous as his public career. His whole
married life was a succession of intrigues, and
several noted personages whose escutcheons bore
the bar sinister traced their ancestry directly to
him. By his children's governess, he is supposed to
have been the father of Madame Cappelle, whose
daughter, Marie Lafarge,* played the stellar rôle
in the most sensational of French murder mysteries; also of that mysterious creature of loveliness, the beloved "Pamela"† who married the
Irish martyr, Lord Edward Fitzgerald. Indeed,

---

*See page 238.
† See page 93.

Philippe Egalite knew no scruple that would thwart expediency.

Therefore, Dame Gossip found ready listeners when she whispered about the chancelleries of Europe that old Philippe's ambitions had been defied by the stork and that a girl, born to him and his wife at the time when a son was devoutly desired, had been smuggled away and a boy substituted in her place. According to the story, this infant daughter, cheated out of her rightful place as a princess of the realm, was allowed to follow the career of a ballet dancer, although later partly compensated by marriage to a wealthy nobleman.

King Louis Philippe, according to this story, was the boy substituted for her—an Italian peasant child, one Chiappini, the son of a jailer who was paid well for having his baby placed in line for accession to the throne of France. The Citizen King's democratic ways and sincere espousal of the people's cause were supposed to have resulted from this plebeian blood.

Whether the story was true or not, old Czar Nicholas placed his stamp of approval upon it, for once, in a moment of wrath, he exclaimed sneeringly of King Louis Philippe:

"He is a common jailer's son!"

CHAPTER II

Mysteries of Six Famous Queens

Cleopatra—How Did She Die?

FOR her actual beauty, it is said, was not in itself so remarkable that none could be compared with her, or that no one could see her without being struck by it, but the contact of her presence, if you lived with her, was irresistible; the attraction of her person, joining with the charm of her conversation, and the character that attended all she said or did, was something bewitching. It was a pleasure merely to hear the sound of her voice, with which, like an instrument of many strings, she could pass from one language to another; so that there were few of the barbarian nations that she answered by an interpreter."

In these words did Plutarch describe Cleopatra, the last queen of Egypt, daughter of Ptolemy Auletes.

This arch-temptress of all the ages was born at Alexandria, Egypt, sixty-nine years B. C., and with her brother Ptolemy became joint ruler over Egypt when she was a sprightly girl

of eighteen.   After having enjoyed a reign of but
three years she was dethroned by her brother's
partisans.   While their respective armies were
preparing for war, Cæsar arrived in Egypt and
reinstated her upon her throne.   Then followed
a liaison between the young Queen of the Nile
and the middle-aged conqueror of the world.   It
lasted until there was born to them a son, Cesar-
ion, and during two years afterward, at which
time Cleopatra lived with Cæsar in Rome, not
returning to Egypt until after his murder in the
Senate.   Three years later the calm of the siren
of the Nile was to be again disturbed by a noble
Roman—this time the handsome and dashing
Mark Antony, who had been appointed ruler of
Asia and the East.   Being summoned before
Antony to answer accusations of having aided his
enemies, Cleopatra came sailing to him in "a
barge with gilded stern and outspread sails of
purple, while oars of silver beat time to the music
of flutes and fifes and harps.   She herself lay all
alone under a canopy of cloth of gold, dressed
as Venus in a picture, and beautiful young boys,
like painted cupids, stood on each side to fan her.
Her maids were dressed like sea nymphs and
graces, some steering at the rudder, some working at the ropes."

As a result of this excursion Antony became

her captive instead of her captor. "Were Antony serious or disposed to mirth," says Plutarch, "she had at any moment some new delight or charm to meet his wishes; at every turn she was upon him, and let him escape her neither by day nor by night. She played at dice with him, drank with him, hunted with him; and when he exercised in arms, she was there to see."

As a result of this adventure Antony divorced his wife, the sister of the Emperor Augustus, which resulted in the Emperor's declaring war on Cleopatra. The fleet of Antony and Cleopatra was defeated by that of Augustus when the little queen was thirty-eight years old. She fled from the Romans, followed by her lover, who, on hearing a false report of her death, killed himself.

To make Augustus's triumph complete it was decreed that Cleopatra should be exhibited in Rome, but she thwarted these arrangements. Visiting the monument which sheltered Antony's tomb, she shut herself up therein with only her two maids of honor. She wrote to the Emperor a letter, making pathetic entreaties that she might be buried in the tomb with Antony. Later, when some soldiers opened the doors of the monument, they found the beautiful Cleopatra dead, "lying upon a bed of gold, set out in all her royal ornaments." Her two maids, by her side, were in a dying condition.

As to how Cleopatra met her death has for centuries been one of the riddles of the sphinx. One story was that just before she shut herself in the tomb a countryman bearing a basket of figs was allowed to pass the guards and enter her presence with an asp hidden under the fruit. By allowing this serpent to sting her—some say upon the arm, others aver upon the bosom—she is alleged to have committed suicide. According to another account, she kept the asp in a vase and with a golden spindle tantalized it until it stung her. Another story was that she killed herself with poison carried in a hollow bodkin upon which she wound her wonderful hair.

But it has been argued that if she had chosen any serpent to sting her it would have been the small viper rather than the large asp. Moreover, it is related that she was found dead "without any mark or suspicion of poison on her body," and that a serpent's bite would have left an unmistakable blemish. Many authorities have argued that Cleopatra's vanity would never have allowed her to select a mode of death that would have disfigured her so frightfully as a serpent's sting.

"What really took place is known to no one," says Plutarch.

The Secret of Queen Elizabeth

Locked in the depths of Queen Elizabeth's heart was a dark secret that no one could ever fathom.   Various biographers have remarked upon her secretiveness, and upon the fact that she took very few people into her confidence.

She never married.   Those who have written her history have expressed their amazement at her attitude toward men.   At various times she averred that she would never take unto herself a husband.   When only fifteen, and while being ardently courted by Lord Admiral Seymour (who later wedded her stepmother, Queen Catherine Parr), she wrote to that suitor a letter, in which she stated in regard to the possibility of her future marriage: ". . . if ever I should think of it (which I do not believe), you would be the first to whom I should make known my resolution." When she was twenty-three, Giovanni Michiel, the Venetian Ambassador, wrote of her to the Doge of Venice: "She, I understand, having plainly said that she will not marry, even were they to give her the King's" (Philip of Spain's) "son, or find any other great prince, I again respectfully remind your serenity to enjoin secrecy about this."

She would not allow physicians to examine her even when she was seriously ill.   She looked upon them as a source of danger.

Her masculinity was a subject of comment. "The constitution of her mind is exempt from female weakness, and she is endowed with an excellent power of application," her tutor, Roger Ascham, wrote of her in a letter to the rector of Strasbourg University, when she was seventeen. "In the whole manner of her life," added Ascham, "she rather resembles Hippolyta" (Queen of the Amazons) "than Phaedra" (who was wont to love not wisely, but too well).

She carried about with her a stock of wigs— "no less than eighty of various colors." She bore no resemblance to her alleged mother, Anne Boleyn, although she was said by some biographers to favor her father, King Henry VIII.

The only persons who enjoyed her confidence were her childhood nurse, Mrs. Ashley, and the King's cofferer, or steward, Thomas Parry.

When Elizabeth was only fifteen, Sir Robert Tyrwhit, the great English critic, wrote of her to Protector Somerset: "I do verily believe that there hath been some secret promise between my lady, Mistress Ashley, and the cofferer never to confess to death, and if it be so, it will never be gotten unless by the King's Majesty, or else by your Grace." To the end of her days she was loyal to Parry and Mrs. Ashley. On her accession to the throne, she appointed Parry Controller of the Royal Household. She continued to shower honors upon both him and his daughter as long as they lived—"conduct," remarks the biographer, Strickland, "which naturally induces the suspicion that secrets of great moment had been confided to him—secrets that probably would have touched not only the maiden name of his royal mistress, but placed her life in jeopardy, and that he had preserved these inviolate. The same may be supposed with respect to Mrs. Ashley, to whom Elizabeth clung with unshaken tenacity through every storm." After succeeding to the throne, Elizabeth knighted Parry. During Mrs. Ashley's last illness she was honored by personal attentions from the Queen, who mourned her old nurse with deep grief.

What was this secret which Elizabeth guarded so closely, and which seems to have been shared by these two functionaries of the royal household? Only within the last decade has an answer of any definiteness ever been ventured by an authority daring to confide it to the world at large.

Upon the eastern slope of Cotswold Hills, in 'Gloucestershire, lies hidden the ancient village of Bisley, at whose manor house, Overcourt, Elizabeth, when a child of eleven, was isolated in charge of Mrs. Ashley during a pestilence, which threatened London.

The author, Bram Stoker, some time ago, visited Bisley, and uncovered this tradition: During the child Elizabeth's stay in the village she died of a sudden illness upon the eve of a visit from her father, Henry VIII. In terror, Mrs. Ashley placed the Princess' body in a stone tomb, and scoured the country round for a child resembling Elizabeth sufficiently well to allow a substitution that would deceive the King, who had never taken the trouble to acquaint himself very familiarly with his fair-haired daughter. Unable to find a girl bearing sufficient likeness, the nurse discovered a boy of the name of Neville, strikingly like Elizabeth in appearance. This lad, the story ran, was dressed in the Princess' clothes, and masqueraded as the royal child thenceforth throughout the career of the personage known in history as Queen Elizabeth. According to this tradition, all persons learning the secret, except Mrs. Ashley and Thomas Parry, were "gotten rid of."

Some years ago, when a stone tomb upon the estate of Overcourt was opened, the bones of a young girl were found therein lying among remnants of costly clothing. Mr. Stoker has suggested that the boy, masquerading as the royal princess and later as Queen Elizabeth, was a son born at an inopportune time to Henry

VIII's natural son, the Duke of Richmond, and Mary Howard, whom he married.

Whether or not these traditions and speculations have any foundation in fact, the world may never know, and probably the deep secret of Queen Elizabeth will remain unanswered until the end of time.

The Riddle of Mary, Queen of Scots

"Farewell, France, farewell! I shall never see thee more!"

A beautiful girl of nineteen, ensconced upon a couch, wistfully viewed the retreating French coast from the deck of a vessel which was bearing her back to her native Scotland. She was Mary Stuart, who, upon the death of her father, James V, had been crowned Queen of Scots when a child of only ten months, and who, after having been especially educated in France for a marriage with the Dauphin had wedded that princeling when she was only sixteen. A year later her husband ascended the French throne, but her reign as Queen of France had in another year been cut short by his untimely death. And now this spirited girl, still in her teens, was both Dowager Queen of the French and reigning Queen of Scotland.

The depression which Queen Mary suffered on

seeing her beloved France fade from her sight was a shadow cast upon her soul by coming events. Immediately upon landing in Scotland she became involved in quarrels with her people because of her adherence to the Catholic faith, in which she had been reared. And she was drawn into a dispute with her cousin, Queen Elizabeth of England, whose legitimacy was disputed and whose throne was claimed for the young Queen of Scots. But Queen Mary's worst troubles began when her uncles set about to find for her a second husband. After divers nobles had been suggested to her, she was finally persuaded to share her throne with Lord Darnley, son of the Earl of Lennox, but after their marriage she discovered him to be a vicious weakling, and her justified contempt for him aroused his bitter jealousy. Suspecting her attachment for David Rizzio, her French secretary, the King had the foreigner assassinated under her very eyes.

This crime but increased the Queen's contempt for her consort, and thereafter her friendship with the Earl of Bothwell became the subject of comment.

Bothwell aided Mary Stuart when all others seemed to desert her and she clung to his strong arm. But, unfortunately for them both, the

young King was just at this precarious time blown
up with gunpowder while alone in a house.
Bothwell, after having been tried and acquitted
of this murder, was recommended by the nobility
to become the Queen's husband, but, returning
with her suite to Edinburgh, he threw ceremony
to the winds, and, like Lochinvar, carried her off
by force to his castle at Dunbar.   Then, obtaining
a hurried divorce from his wife, he married Queen
Mary a few days afterward.   Thereupon the
Scotch nobles, outraged by the adventure, raised
a rebellion against their Queen and locked her up
in Lochlevin Castle.   But she escaped to England to seek the protection of her cousin Elizabeth.

Her abdication was forced and her evil half-
brother, James Stuart, Earl of Murray, illegitimate son of King James, was now made regent
for her infant son.

By escaping into England Mary Stuart had
but fallen from the frying pan into the fire.
Queen Elizabeth, still smarting from her cousin's
former claim to the English throne, decided that
she must investigate certain charges that Mary
had conspired with Bothwell to assassinate her
second husband, Darnley—charges that had been
made by the Earl of Murray, who, of course,
wished to retain her throne.   As proofs of her
guilt, Murray placed before a commission of

inquiry a silver casket alleged to have been given
to Mary by her first husband, the young King of
France, and to have been later given by her to
Bothwell.   It contained love letters and sonnets
said to have been written in her own hand to
that lord; also two papers, one in her own hand
and one subscribed by her.

These letters, if genuine, contained incontest-
able proofs of a criminal correspondence between
Mary and Bothwell, of her consent to Darnley's
murder and of her concurrence in Bothwell's
plot to kidnap her and carry her off.   Claiming
this evidence to have been forged, Mary instructed
her commissioners to ignore it.   And since then
Great Britain has been divided into two camps,
those believing that she wrote the celebrated
"casket letters" and those believing them to
have been spurious.   Although these letters had
enjoined Bothwell to burn them, he had—'twas
alleged—foolishly committed them to the custody
of the deputy governor of Edinburgh Castle, who,
in revenge for a later slight, had allowed one of
Murray's henchmen to intercept them.

By those who have believed Mary guilty it
has been argued that her evil half-brother,
Murray, would not have staked his success on
forgeries destined to pass muster before many
shrewd investigators; that the verbosity of the

letters proved their genuineness; that they contained particulars which nobody else would have thought to invent; that they detailed a conversation between Mary and the murdered King that was afterward recalled by a gentleman as having been related to him by the King, and that the Duke of Norfolk was fully convinced of her guilt.

On the other hand, it seemed absurd that any one so shrewd as Mary Stuart should have confided such indiscretions to paper; that any one so wily as Bothwell should have preserved incriminating evidence against himself, and that the Duke of Norfolk, if convinced of her having murdered her second husband, would have later so zealously tried to become her fourth consort. Furthermore, investigation of charters and deeds signed by Queen Mary showed that she was not in the places mentioned in the famous letters on the days assigned therein.

Moreover, Mary was a clever poet, and the sonnets credited to her were crude and inelegant. She was a woman of refinement—who conducted even her amours as a lady—and the letters attributed to her were to the last degree indecent as well as written in a crude style to which she never could have descended.

Later the casket letters mysteriously disappeared. Some said that they were destroyed by friends of her son, the boy King James, that every evidence of his mother's supposed indiscretions might be erased.

Whether genuine or not, the "casket letters" certainly helped to pave Queen Mary's way to the scaffold.

The truth concerning them will ever remain buried in the black heart of the mysterious past.

The Mystery of Empress Catherine I

Early in the eighteenth century an illiterate girl with the figure and bearing of a peasant, but a good nature and charm that made her irresistible to men, resided in the home of Prince Menshikoff, the favorite of Czar Peter the Great.

The Czar, visiting the Prince in 1703, met this mysterious creature, fell despeartely in love with her at first sight and took her from his subject. Martha—for such was her name—soon became so indispensable to the ruler of her land that he found it a torment to be separated from her, and henceforth throughout his life she was his inseparable companion, even during his military campaigns. She shared the perils and hardships of his various wars, calmed the wild outbreaks of his savage temper, and during his Caspian campaigns she was obliged to shear off her beautiful hair that she might endure the fierce rays of the sun

while in the field with him.   During his dis-
astrous campaign in Turkey, when he faced the
alternative of starving on the banks of the Pruth
or of ignominiously surrendering his army, Martha
cleverly saved him by bribing the Turkish Grand
Vizier with her jewels.

For his sake she adopted the Greek Catholic
faith, and with it the name Catherine Alexievna.
Two years after she had borne him a daughter—
which, in her honor, he named Catherine—the
Czar privately married her, whereafter she presented him with another daughter, Anna (later
the Duchess of Holstein-Gottorp, mother of
Peter III), and in 1709 a third child, Elizabeth,
who lived to be Empress of Russia.

Although secretly married to Catherine, Peter
the Great already had a lawful wife, the Czarina
Eudoxia.   But he divorced his consort in 1711
and afterward publicly acknowledged Catherine
as his consort.   In 1718 he declared her Empress
and in 1722 proclaimed her his successor to the
throne—to the exclusion of the little Grand Duke
Peter, his six-year-old son by his divorced wife.
As Empress-consort, Peter had Catherine crowned
at Moscow in 1724, her crown worn during the
ceremony being studded with 2564 precious
stones and surmounted by a ruby, as large as a
pigeon's egg, supporting a cross of brilliants.

On the eve of her coronation she was threatened
with ruin by suspicions of an intrigue between her
and her gentleman-of-the-bedchamber, William
Moens.   Although believing her to be innocent,
Peter had Moens' head lopped off and placed in
her apartment preserved in a jar of alcohol, where
it might warn her of the fate that would befall
any of his future rivals.   At the same time Moens'
sister was cruelly flogged and his two sons sent
away to Persia.   When shown the head of her
alleged cavalier, Catherine asserted calmly:

"What a pity the people of the court are so
corrupt!"

Whether Catherine was guilty or innocent of
this intrigue historians have never been able to
agree, but in spite of the scandal she strengthened
her position with Peter to the extent of not only
gaining her crown, but of having him reinstate in
his favor her former lover, Menshikoff, in whose
house he had met her.   The Czar expired in her
arms during January, 1725, and the fact that she
kept his death secret until after securing her succession to the throne gave rise to suspicions that
she had poisoned him; but the Archbishop of
Pskov declared under oath to the people and to
the army that Peter upon his death bed had
designated Catherine as his successor.   So the
people of Russia gave their allegiance to the first

Empress who had ever ruled over them. Selecting Menshikoff as her chief adviser, she entered upon a reign which, at the end of two years, was cut short by death, due to her intemperate habits.

Who Catherine I was she herself, perhaps, never knew. Her mother was undoubtedly a serf, but as to the identity of her father there are several theories. One is that he was a Baltic nobleman, Colonel Rosen; another that he was a small Catholic yeoman of Lithuanian stock, Samuel Skovionsky, who died of the plague while she was a baby. According to a third account, she was the daughter of a Swedish quartermaster, John Rabe.

Perhaps not even her mother knew which of these theories was correct. At any rate, the child was left an orphan in the village of Lavonia, where she was taken care of first by the sexton of the place and later by a Protestant clergyman, named Gluck, superintendent of Marienburg, who educated her with his children, but whose wife endeavored to rid herself of Martha by marrying her off to a Swedish dragoon, one Johan.

After the capture of Marienburg Martha and Johan became forever separated, and, with the family of Parson Gluck, she was made a captive by a Russian general, who, although he treated the old clergyman kindly, retained all the women

of his household.   At the distribution of the
spoils he allotted Martha, then a girl of seventeen,
to General Bauer, whose mistress she remained
until ceded to Prince Menshikoff.

Such was the history of the most enigmatical
woman who ever sat upon a European throne.

Marie Antoinette and the Diamond Necklace

The Cardinal de Rohan, Grand Almoner of
France, lived in morbid dread of Queen Marie
Antoinette's disfavor.   His troubles had begun
when that hapless Queen once mercilessly snubbed
him at court and he was willing to pay any price
for restoration to her favor.   His plight was one
which naturally opened up a fertile field for
blackmailers and that class of adventurers who
take advantage of persons in trouble.   Cagliostro,
the celebrated magician, in return for a substantial
fee, assured the Cardinal that he had used his
mystic powers to regain the Queen's good will.
Another agent employed by de Rohan to obtain
her Majesty's forgiveness was the Countess de la
Motte, a cousin of the King.   Coming to him
with the claim that she could effect a reconcilia-
tion, the Countess had obtained various sums of
money from the Cardinal for that purpose.

The late King, the dissolute Louis XV, had
ordered for his mistress, the Countess Du Barry,

a diamond necklace, valued at a third of a million
dollars, but had died before it had been finished
by the jewelers. It later changed hands several
times and eventually fell into the possession of a
firm of Paris jewelers, who, about the time of the
Cardinal's employment of the Countess de la
Motte, were attempting to sell it to the Queen.
But Marie Antoinette rejected it, stating that it
was ugly and not to her taste. While the jewelers
were nursing their disappointment the Countess
de la Motte entered their establishment and in-
formed them that Marie Antoinette really wanted
the diamond necklace very badly and hesitated
to take it openly because she feared that the purchase would further embitter the common people,
who were already railing against her extravagance.
The Countess, according to her story, had been
appointed as the Queen's secret agent to negotiate
the purchase and, leaving the jeweler's shop, she
went straightway to Cardinal de Rohan, telling
him the same story and assuring him that his
favor with the Queen would surely be restored if
he would covertly arrange to order the necklace
for her, it being agreed that Marie Antoinette
should remit for it in four quarterly payments.
The Cardinal jumped at the opportunity, and in
his presence the jewelers delivered the necklace
to the Countess, who turned it over to a man who,

the Cardinal was given to understand, was a
secret messenger from the Queen.

The Cardinal was soon afterward shown by the
Countess a number of letters alleged to be from the
Queen and greatly complimenting him. Shortly
afterward, the Countess delighted him greatly
by stating that the Queen desired to meet him
secretly in a grove on a certain night. The
Cardinal proceeded to the place mentioned and
there met a heavily cloaked figure, who presented him with a rose and whispered:

"You may hope that the past is forgotten."

But in spite of all this evidence that the Countess
had, in truth, bought for him the Queen's favor
with the generous funds that he had given to her,
de Rohan's troubles now began to multiply. He
anxiously awaited the Queen's appearance, wearing the necklace, but noted with alarm that she
never adorned herself with it. Nor did she relax
her cold demeanor toward him at court; nor
were his fortunes advanced in any way. Worst
of all, the promised quarterly remittances for the
diamond necklace were not forthcoming from her
majesty. Entering the palace chapel one morning, clothed in his full regalia, and prepared to say
high mass, Rohan was apprehended by the King.
It appeared that the jewelers, tired of waiting for
their money, had commenced to dun the Queen

directly, and that she had referred the bill to the King, protesting her ignorance of the charge. The Cardinal made a clean breast of the whole matter to the King, and Marie Antoinette hearing the confession, flew into a rage, branding the Cardinal as a scoundrel. Poor de Rohan, realizing that he had been duped by someone, offered to pay for the necklace out of his own pocket, but the Queen demanded his arrest, and the King signed the warrant.

His trial before Parliament lasted for nine months and stirred all France. The revelations of court intrigue and extravagance which it brought forth hastened the Reign of Terror. Those who heard the evidence could never agree as to whether the Countess de la Motte was really the Queen's secret agent or merely an imposter; whether the letters complimenting de Rohan were really from the Queen or skilful forgeries; whether the man to whom the diamond necklace was given was acting for the Countess or the Queen, and whether it was Marie Antoinette or some one impersonating her who received the Cardinal in the grove at night.

According to the Queen's witnesses she was, without her knowledge, impersonated in the grove by a certain Mlle. d'Oliva.

The trial ended in the acquittal of de Rohan

and the public whipping of the Countess de la Motte, who was also branded and sent to prison for a brief term; but the fact that she was allowed unusual luxuries in prison and that d'Oliva was allowed to go scot-free caused many to think that these two women were scapegoats.

The truth as to the diamond necklace will ever remain one of the unfathomable riddles of the court of France.

The Riddle of Empress Tsu-Hsi

A beautiful girl, tall, large-eyed and finely formed, entered the harem of the Chinese Emperor, Hsien-Feng. Not only by her beauty but by her cleverness and charm she attracted the attention of the Emperor's mother and of his first wife, and as a result she became a favorite in the household. Soon she was promoted to the rank of fourth wife, and when the second wife died she took her place.

Two years after entering the imperial harem, Tsu-Hsi—for such was her name—gave birth to a son, and as the Emperor's first wife was childless, this boy, at his father's death, five years later, succeeded to the throne. The first wife and Tsu-Hsi were made coregents for the boy Emperor and each was given the title of Dowager Empress, the former being known therafter as the Empress of the Eastern Palace and Tsu-Hsi as the Empress of the Western Palace.

The Empress of the Eastern Palace was a woman of quiet tastes and retiring disposition, interested mostly in literary pursuits and gifted with no executive ability, while Tsu-Hsi had an active interest in politics and affairs—was made of the metal out of which stern and shrewd rulers are wrought. Being opposites in disposition, the two empresses got along amicably and fostered for each other a sincere affection, which had not been diminshed when the Empress of the Eastern Palace died, in 1881.

Tsu-Hsi suffered a terrible shock when her son, the young Emperor, succumbed to an ominously brief and mysterious illness. But, undaunted by her great grief, she outwitted the mandarins by snatching from his cradle at midnight a three-year-old boy, Kwang-Hsu, first cousin of the dead Emperor, and by hurrying this infant into the council chamber, where she presented him as the new ruler of the empire. It is said that the mandarins protested, but that Tsu-Hsi quelled their objections with blows from a whip. She continued her regency thereafter as foster-mother of the Emperor, who, to the day of his death, she is said to have spanked whenever he expressed his own opinions too emphatically.

The origin of Tsu-Hsi has always been shrouded in mystery as black as that cloaking the indentity of Catherine I, of Russia. To efface all knowledge of her childhood she is said to have forbidden its mention. Members of her court when asked as to her pedigree and childhood always made one answer, "We never discuss the early history of her Majesty."

One story was that Tsu-Hsi was the daughter of a lieutenant-general of the Manchu forces, who was a member of the highest Manchu nobility and that when in her late teens she had entered the imperial palace, not as a concubine, but as a noble guest of the then Dowager Empress. According to another account she was the daughter of Chao, a small military official, afterward raised to the rank of duke, but finally beheaded for some military delinquency. Then there was a tradition that her father was a Tartar general, who died at his post on the River Yang Tze, leaving an indigent widow and two daughters. The widow is said to have been on her way to Pekin, bearing his coffin in a mourning boat decorated with the customary blue and white lanterns, when, on reaching Hankow, she suddenly found herself without funds. According to this story the servants of a local official mistook her boat for that of the governor of the provinee and left upon it rich gifts of gold and viands. The widow in gratitude for the supposed tribute to herself then gave her elder daughter to the local official as a gift and proceeded to Pekin with the younger girl, Wehonala, whom she presented as a candidate for the imperial harem, and who, on being accepted by the Emperor, was given the name Tsu-Hsi.

Still another rumor has it that this most remarkable prodigy of the Mongol race was born a slave girl of low origin and was taken from her native hut on a narrow street inside the eastern gate of Pekin, to be sold in the south of China, where she was found by an official of the court and brought to the palace as one of the sixty concubines of the imperial harem. Her parents are said to have been an itinerant Tartar and a Shanghai dancing girl, and some would have it that they sold her to a Chinese soldier, who had passed her on to a Manchu mandarin. Some say that during the time when she was a slave girl she became acquainted with Li Hung Chang, then in humble position, and that during this friendship neither fostered the hope that they would one day meet in the imperial palace at Pekin, each weighed down with wealth and power.

The fact that Tsu-Hsi's feet were never bound is evidence that she was of humble birth.

The ending of Tsu-Hsi's life was quite as mys-

terious as its beginning. On November 3, 1908,
when she celebrated her seventy-fourth birthday,
she was noticed to be in perfect health; hence
the court was naturally surprised to hear less
than a fortnight later that she had died. At
the same time the announcement was made that
her protégé, the Emperor, had died the day before.
Later evidence indicated that he had given up the
ghost some days previously, but that the fact
had been suppressed. The cause of Tsu-Hsi's
sudden death and the motive for concealing that
of the Emperor are still baffling mysteries.

CHAPTER III

Unsolved Riddles of Four Kings

Don Sebastian, the Vanished King

WHAT is fear?" the young King, Don Sebastian of Portugal, used to ask his courtiers.

It is related that this lion-hearted prince "loved all kinds of danger," that during bloody battles he would run under the guns of his own forts, and that in open boats he would venture out in tempests that caused his shipmates to quake with terror. He was a reckless horseman who, by the pressure of his knees, "could make a powerful horse tremble and sweat." He was also a skilful swordsman. Fatigue was a stranger to him.

Swashbuckling hero that he was, he had yet a feminine face, with delicate features and the complexion of a girl. His hair was reddish gold and his eye a violet blue. No Prince Charming that ever haunted maiden's dreams was braver, bolder or fairer to look upon than this royal youth, and yet it is recorded that he had little time or inclination for affairs of the heart. When he paid court to the Infanta Isabella of Spain he was "as cold as a wooer, as he was ardent as a warrior."

When crowned he was hailed as "another Alexander." He was the popular idol of the Portuguese people, many of whom, even to this day, worship him as a demigod.

Sebastian had been born in 1554 to Prince John and the Princess Juana, who was a daughter of the Emperor Charles V, but his father, not living to succeed to the throne of Portugal, Sebastian, when an infant of three, took the scepter laid down by his grandfather, John III. The tutor who schooled his mind was a Jesuit priest, which accounts for the fact that when he was in his prime he got into his royal head the idea of reviving the Crusades. So he set about to reclaim the Holy Land from the Infidel, and, incidentally, to conquer Morocco. Against the advice of all the wise heads of his domain he recruited an army of 18,000 men, which, together with 6,000 camp followers, embarked in 800 ships and landed on the shores of Morocco in 1578. It was a military expedition de luxe. Sebastian carried with him every luxury that the heart could desire and the appetites crave. There were lists for jousts, a crown which was to be put upon his head when he became King of Morocco and a coterie of poets who were to sing his praises when he should be elevated to the Moroccan throne.

When his army landed therein Morocco was in

the midst of civil war. Sultan Muley was disputing his throne with his nephew Mohammed, and Sebastian conceived the idea of joining forces with the latter, who promised him the aid of four hundred horsemen. Thus resulted what is known in history as "The Battle of the Three Kings," which ended in the disappearance of all of those monarchs from history.

Sebastian did not show good generalship in this adventure. After landing he loitered to enjoy a hunt for big game, and thus allowed the blood of his warriors to cool and the enemy to outwit him. When the fight began he found his 18,000 soldiers opposed by three times as many Moors, and he was ignominiously defeated. This battle was the only one in history in which an army was generaled and led to victory by a dead man. Sultan Muley, upon receiving a mortal wound, fell back upon his litter, ordered the curtain drawn, and cautioned one of his generals to have his corpse borne forward without revealing his death, which was done. Then the general pretended to take his commands from the dead Sultan, inside the litter, thus maintaining the confidence of his troops, who swept the forces of Don Sebastian and Mohammed before them. While retreating across the river Mohammed suffered a less glorious death by drowning and Don Sebastian vanished from the face of the earth, thus leaving behind him one of the great disappearance mysteries of history.

There were many conflicting theories accounting for his fate. One was that after his defeat his corpse, bleeding from seven wounds, was found naked upon the battle-field, taken to Fez and buried, but later returned to Europe and entombed in the Convent of Belen. Others said that he was captured during a brave onslaught and taken prisoner, but recaptured by one of his own generals from whose camp he escaped beyond the Moorish lines to some place from which he never returned. No one ever saw him killed, and it seems certain that had he lain among the dead his luxurious accoutrements would have attracted attention. One persistent story was that, accompanied by a band of brother fugitives, he reached Arzilla. At home Don Sebastian's subjects refused to believe that he had suffered death, and there was a prophecy current among them that he would one day return to deliver them out of their difficulties; this in spite of the fact that his uncle, Cardinal Henry, had been placed upon the throne as his successor.

Six years after Henry's coronation it was announced that Sebastian had been discovered in Spain, but the rumor was alleged to have been circulated in the interests of an impostor, the son of an ignorant potter, who for his pains was sent to the galleys for life, although he later escaped to Paris, where he masqueraded as the Duke of Normandy. Less fortunate were three others who proclaimed themselves the vanished monarch. They were delivered to the executioner, who performed his duty with gruesome variations.

But for generations the Portuguese populace continued to believe that their "hidden king" would return, and even in 1807, during the French invasion of Portugal, these Sebastianists, as they were called, were distributing literature bearing the prophecy that their worshiped hero was about to come out of hiding and destroy Napoleon. Portuguese emigrants to the New World carried this tradition with them, and as late as 1838 there occurred in Brazil a Sebastianist insurrection, fomented by those who still held to the hope that the King who had disappeared two hundred and sixty years before was to return in a ship, which was watched for by many superstitious people, lining the seacoast.

The Mystery of Emperor Frederick

During the year that elapsed between the spring of 1887 and the spring of 1888, the imperial court of Berlin was the scene of mysterious happenings which have since kept the whole world guessing.

William the Great, the first Emperor of the federated German states, was slowly dying. The heir to the throne, the Crown Prince Frederick, was by all odds the most popular man in the empire. In the Franco-Prussian War he had been a great hero, worshiped by his soldiers, who had affectionately dubbed him "Unser (Our) Fritz." At the outbreak of that war, when the loyalty of the south German regiments was in doubt because of their bitter animosity against Prussia, "Unser Fritz" was chosen for their command because it was realized that he was the only power in the empire who could infuse them with enough patriotism to fight. That he was successful is proved by the fact that with these regiments he took Sedan and made a prisoner of Napoleon III.

One of Frederick's biographers, describing his magnetism says:

"Troops commanded by him in person became virtually invincible, for every soldier in the ranks was by the sight of this princely leader stirred to deeds of courage and daring. Even the greatest coward became a hero when he felt the kindly eye of Frederick the Noble upon him."

Like most really strong rulers, Crown Prince Frederick was democratic. Yet, in person he was far more impressive than even his father, William I. Between him and his father there was an

estrangement, as there was also between him and
his son, the lately deposed Kaiser. The old
Emperor regarded Frederick as too liberal in his
views, and Prince Bismarck, the Iron Chancellor,
shared this opinion of the Crown Prince.

A dozen years before the Franco-Prussian War
Frederick had married Queen Victoria's eldest
daughter, the Princess Victoria. The Princess
had become unpopular with the German people.
Her eldest child, the last Kaiser, who was
destined to be dethroned by America and the
Allies, early developed a bumptiousness which
alienated him from his father, himself the most
unaffected and natural of men. Because Frederick had sought to keep his conceited son in the
background until he could be cured of his vanity
the latter never forgave these paternal efforts to
suppress what he considered as God-given cleverness and genius. Indeed, young William, when
only the heir presumptive, accused his father of
being jealous of his own extraordinary talents.

This breach between the Crown Prince and his
son, Prince William, widened early in 1887, when
it was whispered throughout Europe that the
former was suffering from cancer of the throat.
As a matter of fact, following a severe cold,
Frederick had developed in his throat a growth
which was the cause of serious scientific con-

troversy.   Instead of standing by his father in
this grave emergency, Prince William allowed it
to whet his insatiable ambition.   He gathered
about him a strong court faction, which had the
audacity to propose that the afflicted Prince
Frederick's claim to the crown be set aside because
it would be unwholesome to the state of the
empire to have upon the throne a ruler afflicted
with an incurable malady.   Although he realized
that his father, the old Emperor William, was
near unto death, Frederick is said to have signed
a formal pledge that he would abdicate his claims
to the throne in favor of his son, should it be proved
that his malady was incurable.

On hearing of this abdication, Frederick's
English wife, the Crown Princess, became highly
indignant, as justly she might be.   Her husband
was signing away not only his but her own possible
prospects of wearing a monarch's crown.   Her
mother, Queen Victoria, backed her up in her
insistence upon her rights.   So, to contravert her
son's efforts to prove that his father was dying
of cancer, the Crown Princess sent to England for
that country's most eminent throat specialist,
Dr. Morell Mackenzie.

All Europe awaited the diagnosis of this great
savant.   He clipped out a portion of Prince
Frederick's throat tissue and sent it for analysis

to the noted Professor Virchow. Virchow announced that the tissue contained no indications of cancer, and this pronouncement proved a great disappointment to the partisans of Prince William. They immediately accused Doctor Mackenzie of having fraudulently clipped from an unafflicted portion of the Crown Prince's throat the tissue which had been used for the analysis, and Queen Victoria replied to this accusation from her grandson's followers by immediately knighting Doctor Mackenzie. Partisans of the Crown Princess now recommended that Frederick be taken out of Germany to escape the machinations of his German physicians who had been engaged to hasten his end.

Frederick was hurried to England and to San Remo. It was said that young William had become absolutely estranged from both his father and mother, and rumor also had it that Doctor Mackenzie, at the request of the British royal family, was subjecting Frederick to terrible tortures that he might outlive his aged father, if only for a few days.

It was a neck-and-neck race against the Grim Reaper. "Unser Fritz" won. On March 9, 1898, when Kaiser Wilhelm der Grosse gave up the ghost, his dying son was doctored up with stimulants, hurried to Berlin and crowned. He occupied the throne just ninety-nine days.

5

What really happened during those dramatic
months previous to his succession will never be
known.   But the subsequent career of Wilhelm II
proved that he would have fostered no scruple
against the blackest intrigue, even at the expense
of his own father.

The Fate of King Ludwig

"The handsomest man in Europe."

Thus was Ludwig of Bavaria acclaimed when,
at the age of eighteen, he ascended his throne.
A dashing figure, he was popular with his people.
He was known as a young man of deep intellect
and had a decided genius for music and architect-
ure.   When, following the Franco-Prussian War,
the German states united in the one empire,
which the criminal ambitions of William II was
to ruin, it was the eloquent young Ludwig who
made the address offering William of Prussia the
imperial crown.   It was Ludwig also who became
the champion of the great composer, Wagner,
when he was being hounded through Europe and
branded as an anarchist, and Wagner, as a return
for the young king's favor, depicted that ruler as
Parsifal in his great opera of that title.

But Ludwig had not long enjoyed his reign
when evidences of hereditary insanity began to
show themselves in his behavior.   He became

surprisingly extravagant, borrowing millions of dollars with which to build new castles and palaces. Among those who made him such loans were Queen Isabella of Spain and the Khedive of Egypt. He sent emissaries also to the rulers of Austria-Hungary, Brazil, Persia and Sweden, attempting to borrow large sums from them. He surrounded himself with a luxury that almost beggars description. At the door of his private apartments was a solid silver, fruit-laden palm tree, eight feet high, under which crouched the effigy of a horrible dragon.

Ludwig acquired a morbid horror of daylight. After wandering about all night he would retire at daybreak to an artificially darkened apartment and there remain in bed until five in the afternoon. The ceilings of his bedchambers were painted dark blue and studded with pieces of glass cut to represent the moon and stars. Artificial palm trees shaded his bed and the apartment was cooled by an artificial waterfall. During the night his castle, Neuschwannstein, was lighted by eight thousand wax candles, kept burning at a nightly cost of more than one thousand dollars. Thus the ancestral taint of insanity in the royal family began to manifest itself, and it was recalled that Ludwig had had a maniacal outburst at the age of twelve, when he was once interrupted in the

act of gradually strangling his young brother
Otto, who was to succeed him on the throne, and
who also was to become incurably insane.

King Ludwig's chief monomania concerned
Louis XIV of France, on the anniversary of whose
birth each year he would sit down to dinner with
a marble bust of the "Grande Monarque." To this
piece of sculpture he would make extravagant
toasts and speeches. During these celebrations he
would dress as Louis the Grand himself. One
of the rules of his castle was that every one passing
the portrait of Queen Marie Antoinette should
prostrate himself before it, and, to such a height
rose his delirium of grandeur, that he required
all servants waiting on him at table to hand him
his food while on their knees and without daring
to look up at him on pain of being kicked or
having their ears boxed.

Conceiving the idea of selling Bavaria and pur-
chasing a kingdom where his reign might be
absolute, Ludwig dispatched the director of the
Bavarian archives, Doctor Loehr, to the Canary
Islands, Greek Archipelago, Crete, Cyprus and
the Levant in search of a stronghold where his
majesty's sway might be unrestrained during the
remainder of his life; and the unfortunate Doctor
Loehr had to go about on this quixotic mission or
suffer ruin.

By Ludwig's command operas and plays were produced in certain theaters, and when the curtain went up the house would be found empty and dark, the king having forbidden any one but himself to enter; and he would hide somewhere in the shadows, the players never knowing where. Once he became very mad on the subject of "Lohengrin," and sailed about the royal lake garbed as that character of whom he was the prototype. At another time one of his ministers, making an official call at the castle, found the king in his robes of state with his crown cocked over one ear, playing blind-man's buff with a group of stable boys. Complaining of terrible pains in his head, Ludwig at times wore a gutta-percha cap, which he had filled with ice.

Early in 1886 this mad monarch became so troublesome that his ministers had to depose him and place him under restraint in charge of a physician, Doctor Gudden. Castle Berg, on Starnbeg Lake, was converted into a private insane asylum for his majesty. Shortly after being taken there, on June 13, 1886, the mad king's attendants were horrified to find floating in different parts of the lake the corpses of King Ludwig and his physician. How they met their death is a mystery which still vexes Europe.

The Meyerling Tragedy

All of the hopes of Franz-Josef, the late Emperor of Austria-Hungary, were centered in his only son, the Crown Prince Rudolf. This promising young man was married to the Princess Stephanie, daughter of Leopold II, late King of the Belgians, but the union was unhappy. Rudolf was of a lively disposition, care-free, dashing, and fond of adventure, while his wife was moody, sullen and jealous. Thus were supplied two points of the "eternal triangle." The woman in the case was the beautiful young Baroness, Maria Vetsera.

For some time Princess Stephanie had wished a divorce, and Rudolf was willing to supply her with all the necessary legal grounds, but his stern father, the Emperor, forbade such collusion. Rudolf, like his cousin, the Grand Duke Johann Salvator,* offered to relinquish all of his honors for the woman he loved—to give up his rights to the throne if he could but wed Marie Vetsera.

Rudolf arranged a gay house party late in January, 1889. The scene was the castle of Meyerling, twelve miles from Vienna. His beloved Marie was one of the guests. On the morning of January 30th, one of Rudolf's servants entered his bed-chamber and beheld a scene which turned his blood cold. Before him the sole heir to the

---

*See page 227.

throne of Austria-Hungary lay dead.   At first it
was given out that the young Crown Prince during
the night had died of apoplexy, but as he was only
thirty and possessed of a magnificent physique,
this story was not credited by medical men, and
the suspicion became broadcast that the public
was being deceived by the court bulletins.   Later
there was issued an announcement that Rudolf
had committed suicide, and great excitement
resulted.   But a third shock was in store for the
subjects of Franz-Josef.   There gradually leaked
out the fact that the corpse of Baroness Marie
Vetsera had been found with that of the Crown
Prince.

Then followed a long list of conflicting theories
as to the cause of the Meyerling tragedy.   According to one story Rudolf, during the gay house party
at the castle, had told the Baroness of his father's
refusal to allow his divorce, and that she, unwilling
to live without him, had killed herself.   Some say
that she left a note, beseeching him to follow her
into eternity, and that upon finding this he had
covered her corpse with a pall of flowers, had lain
upon the floor beside her couch and blown out his
brains with an army pistol.

According to a further theory, the lovers, as
soon as they discovered their marriage to be
hopeless, had entered upon a suicide pact, that

Rudolf agreed to shoot the Baroness between the shoulder blades, and that he left a note explaining that he had placed the bullet where it "would not mar her beauty."

It was asserted in some quarters that Marie had a fiancé whom she had promised to jilt for Rudolf, that this nobleman was present at the house party, that Rudolf in a fit of jealousy over her attentions to his rival had shot her, that her other suitor had brained Rudolf with a chair, and that the Crown Prince's servants had later killed his slayer.   There was another story that Marie herself had shot Rudolf and had then taken poison.   And it was further related that the Crown Prince while hunting had been shot by a peasant whom he had once subjected to cruelty, whereupon the Baroness Marie, upon seeing his corpse brought back to the castle, had committed suicide from grief.

Some time after the tragedy, a New York newspaper published evidence purporting to prove that Rudolf and his beloved Marie were living in voluntary exile in America under assumed names, and other newspapers have from time to time hinted that the story of the Meyerling tragedy had been a hoax designed to cover up a scandal and enable him to lose himself in foreign lands. Several times in recent years persons have asserted that they had seen Rudolf in various parts of America. An authoritative encyclopedia records its skepticism of the official account of his death by stating that he was "believed" to have taken his own life.

After Rudolf's mysterious death the right of succession to the throne of Austria-Hungary fell to the Emperor's brother, Charles Louis. But, sharing the proverbial "Hapsburg luck," so long a synonym for tragedy, the latter died, leaving the succession to his son, Archduke Francis Ferdinand.

Indeed, throughout his long reign, Franz Josef was a man of sorrows. Shortly after his coronation had come his unhappy marriage with the Princess Elizabeth of Bavaria; their mysterious quarrel, her flight, and their eight years of separation; then the execution of Franz Josef's brother, the Emperor Maximilian, of Mexico; and on top of the terrible Meyerling tragedy came the mysterious disappearance of Franz Josef's nephew, Grand Duke Johann Salvator; the disgrace and banishment of the Emperor's sole surviving brother, Louis Victor; the murder of Franz Josef's consort, the Empress Elizabeth, at Geneva, and finally the assassination of the heir to the throne, the Archduke Francis Ferdinand and the latter's morganatic wife, that crime

which William II of Germany used as a pretext
for starting the bloody European war.

Probably the truth that has lain hidden behind
the Meyerling tragedy for more than a generation
will never be uncovered.   The world knows as
little about it today as it did upon the morning of
its occurrence.

CHAPTER IV

Hidden Victims of Autocracy

The Man of the Iron Mask

UPON the register of the grim Bastille was this entry:

"On Thursday, the 18th of September, 1698, at three o'clock of the afternoon, M. de Saint-Mars, governor of the chateau of the Bastille, arrived for his first entrance into office, coming from his government of the islands of Sainte-Marguerite, having brought with him in his litter a former prisoner of his at Pigneroi, whom he obliges to keep himself always masked, and whose name is not told."

Instant death was the penalty the mysterious prisoner must pay should he ever reveal his face— this by royal command of Louis the Grand; he who boasted, "I am the State!"

It had been seventeen years since M. de Saint-Mars had left Pigneroi with his masked prisoner, who, meanwhile, had languished in the dungeons of Sainte-Marguerite. So when that mysterious man arrived at the Bastille he had already endured his tortures through a period in which many a maker of history has lived his lifetime.

'Twas rumored that his features had to be forever hidden because they bore a resemblance that was compromising to the grand monarch. He must have been a personage of great rank. His jailers were commanded to treat him always with that respect which was due to royalty alone. Even M. de Saint-Mars himself had to stand bareheaded when addressing his charge.

The mask was of black velvet, another entry in the prison register stated. According to Voltaire it had steel springs at the chin piece, allowing the wearer to eat without uncovering his face; but this detail is supposed to have been one of the fruits of Voltaire's vivid imagination. Yet its suggestion yielded up the name, "Man of the Iron Mask," by which the unfortunate sufferer has since been known to history and to fiction.

He languished in the cruel Bastille five years two months and one day. Then his tortured soul went up to his Creator, relieved of a hell of torment known to have lasted for at least twenty-two years and which probably had covered a longer period of agony. It left behind no clue as to his identity or his antecedents. Only M. de Saint-Mars and the grand monarch could tell; and their lips were sealed until the Black Angel delivered them out of the tortures which their conscience must have endured on their victim's account.

For a dozen years after the masked prisoner had died not even M. de Saint-Mars' brothers in arms, who had helped to guard that wretched existence, dared to ask themselves who their prisoner might have been. Then Louis XIV went up for his final judgment after more than seventy years upon his throne, and men dared to gossip behind closed doors. But the first published attempt to unravel the mystery was ventured only after that cruel monarch had been molding in his tomb for a generation. This was in the anonymous "Memoirs" of an author supposed to have been an intriguing court belle. According to this authority, the masked man had been the Duc de Vermandois, natural son of Louis XIV by the beautiful Louise de la Valliere. During an outburst of anger he had dared strike the Dauphin and had suffered a lifetime of torture for this attack upon the heir to the throne.

Voltaire, in his "Century of Louis XVI," later presented another key to the mystery, of which he said: "It is without example, and, what is no less strange, all historians have been ignorant of it." Shortly after 1661, when Cardinal Mazarin died and Louis XIV took the government into his own hands, "a prisoner of greater than ordinary stature, young and of most handsome and noble form, was sent under strict secrecy to the island of Sainte-Marguerite," Voltaire went on to relate. The king's minister, Louvois, went to see the prisoner on the island and spoke to him, standing, with every sign of respect. According to this author, the prisoner was a half-brother of Louis XIV, the son of that monarch's mother, "Haughty" Anne of Austria, and of Mazarin.

This disclosure was shortly followed by a pamphlet emphatically stating that this natural son of Anne and Mazarin had been put on the throne by Mazarin in substitution for the real Louis XIV; that the personage who for more than seventy years enjoyed all of the prestige of "The Grand Monarch" was, therefore, a pseudo king, and that the unknown prisoner of the Bastille was the rightful ruler of France. According to a further theory that prisoner was a half-brother of Louis the Grand, but his father was the English Duke of Buckingham, and not Cardinal Mazarin. Others have maintained that he was a twin brother of the grand monarch and had been put away to avoid complications—the theory seized upon by Dumas for the plot of his novel, "The Man in the Iron Mask."

There was once circulated a story that this man

of mystery had been the rightful Louis XIV, that
he had been married upon the island of Sainte-
Marguerite to his jailer's daughter and that there
had been born to this union a son who was smuggled over to Corsica, where his foster parents were
simply told that he "came from good part,"
which assurance translated into Italian gave him
the name "Buonaparte."   He was the grandfather of the great Napoleon, who thus, in the
third generation, came forward to avenge the
sins of the fathers!

That the Man of the Iron Mask was a personage
of less than royal blood has been maintained in
more recent years; but these theories do not
account for the fact that he was treated with the
deference due only to blood royal.   Some authorities claim that he was the French officer, Bulonde,
who had displeased his royal master during a
military siege; others that he was M. de Marchiel,
a French soldier of fortune who led a conspiracy
for the assassination of Louis XIV; that he was
Count Mattioli,* the Duke of Mantua's Minister
of State, who left a disappearance mystery behind
him, and that he was that human enigma, James
de la Cloche, that son of Charles II of England,
who dissolved into nothingness about the time
that the Man of the Iron Mask appears to have

*See page 75.

been placed in confinement at Pigneroi and whose strange story we will next relate.

James de la Cloche—The Near-King Who Vanished

When that Prince of Wales who became King Charles II of England was a lad barely eighteen he enjoyed a romance upon the Isle of Jersey. Some authorities state that a secret morganatic marriage resulted, others that the affair was a mere adventure. Whatever its status, a child resulted—a son, who assumed the name James de la Cloche. There were persistent rumors that the lad's mother was Marguerite de Cartaret, who, with her brother, Sir George Cartaret, dwelt in the beautiful old Manoir de la Trinite, in the isle above mentioned. The young prince and his brother, the Duke of York, were entertained there by Sir George, to whom Charles, when King, gave what is now our State of New Jersey, named in honor of that Eden which had such a warm place in the royal memory.

In any event, James de la Cloche is known to have been recognized by Charles II as his son. His royal father had him educated in France and granted him a pension of £500 a year, which was to continue so long as he remained a Protestant— this proviso being more on account of its political

effect than any strict aversion borne by the King
to the Catholic faith, for His Majesty was at
heart a Romanist.

In several letters Charles II expressed his purpose to one day publicly recognize his son.   He
further hinted that he might declare that youth
his rightful heir to the throne, for Charles II and
his Queen had no issue; and neither had the Duke
of York, at that time.   King Charles stipulated
to James de la Cloche that he must not reveal his
parentage until his recognition should be openly
made, but the young man disobeyed this command by confiding in Queen Christina of Sweden,
whom he met at Hamburg.   Subsequently he proceeded to Rome bearing with him a letter written by
Her Majesty in Latin and attesting that Charles
II had privately acknowledged him to be his son.

In Rome James de la Cloche chose to further
disobey his royal sire and to forfeit his comfortable pension by joining the Jesuit order and
by entering one of its monasteries when he was
twenty-two years old.   But King Charles, instead .
of seeking to punish his offspring for this defiance,
either forgave him forthwith or affected so to do,
for not long afterward he sent a secret message
to Olivia, general of the Jesuits, confessing that
his heart craved Catholicism and asking that the
young Jesuit, James de la Cloche, be sent to him

6

to instruct him in the faith.   About the same
time James received from his father a letter
addressing him as:

"Our Honored Son, the Prince Stuart, dwelling
under the name of Signor de la Cloche."

So, in the autumn of 1668, de la Cloche, in
disguise and under an assumed name, proceeded
to London to see the King, bearing with him the
belief that he might one day sit upon the British
throne, should he see fit to leave the militant
order of the Church of Rome.   But King Charles
was not yet ready to acclaim him to the multitude as his son and heir.   Instead he wished to
make use of James as a secret messenger between
him and his ally, the Pope.

The message which de la Cloche was to bear
gave assurances to the Holy See that Charles II,
his sister, Duchess Henriette of Orleans, and Louis
XIV of France had conspired to wage war against
Holland   and   restore   Roman   Catholicism   in
England.

In the month following that of his return to
England, James left London with this confidence,
whose betrayal would have wrecked his father's
throne and his own chances of succession thereto.
While proceeding back to Rome he became lost
to history, and no one has since learned what
became of him.

All that has accounted for his fate after he took leave of his father, at the British court, has been mere theory and speculation. Some authorities believed that he was murdered by some one who was jealous over the royal favor shown to him while he was being entertained at court; others that one of his servants assassinated him.

Shortly after his strange disappearance there appeared at Naples a dissolute swindler and impostor, who masqueraded under the name of Giacopo Stuardo, and there was a story that this adventurer was de la Cloche. But inasmuch as that young man was a pious youth who had every reason to serve his masters well, who might look to the West for a throne, or to the East for ecclesiastical honors, this theory was absurd. Another was that the adventurer Stuardo was not de la Cloche, after all, but the servant who had assassinated him and had proceeded for part of his journey under his dead master's name.

Some have advanced the belief that James de la Cloche was disposed of by no less a personage than his own royal sire; that while bearing back to Rome the news of the conspiracy to recatholicize England the young man had somewhere committed the indiscretion of sharing this confidence with some one, as he had confided his parentage to the Queen of Sweden.

According to this theory, King Charles, on hearing of his son's betrayal of his confidence, trembled with the fear that the story might get abroad, that the Protestants in England might again rise in their bloody wrath, and that his head, like his father's, might fall by the axe. Consequently he gave the alarm to his "great and good friend," Louis XIV, who had James de la Cloche arrested and placed in prison, where he became that mysterious personage, "The Man of the Iron Mask."

But that is all speculation, and the world can as yet but guess at the fate of this young man, who might have become King of England.

The Lost Dauphin

The fall of the guillotine upon the neck of Louis XVI made that hapless monarch's only son, the Dauphin Charles Louis, King of France.

The child king was shut up in the prison of the Temple at the time of his father's execution. He was not yet eight years old and altogether at the mercy of his jailer, Simon, a member of the Consell Generale de la Seine, who had orders from the Terrorists to teach the helpless lad indecent and profane language and to make a drunkard of him. After languishing in prison for three years the little King Louis XVII became lost to history.

His fate has been one of the sphinx riddles of the ages. Every one sharing knowledge of it seems to have come to a tragic end. Simon, the jailer, had his head lopped off by the guillotine, leaving the secret to his widow, Mme. Simon, who, by order of King Louis XVIII, was seized immediately after the Bourbon restoration and imprisoned in an insane asylum at Bictere until her death, fifteen years later. She had persisted in asserting that the boy king had been carried off, and it is claimed that her imprisonment was directly due to her knowledge of the lad's fate. The Abbe Dubois, rector of St. Marguerite's, was commanded by Louis XVIII to sign a declaration that the remains of the lost child had been interred in the cemetery of that church and on refusing to comply was poisoned to death. The Duc de Berri, nephew of Louis XVIII, asserted that the boy king still lived, and after denouncing his royal uncle as a usurper suffered assassination.

In 1810 there appeared in Berlin a mysterious stranger, who, in the upper part of his face, bore an astonishing resemblance to Louis XVI and had the famous protruding chin characteristic of Marie Antoinette's family. Claiming to be the lost Dauphin, he correctly described secret hiding places in the interior of the Temple prison, where the boy king had been confined and

went into elaborate details concerning plots
to rescue the royal child.   Bearing upon these
plots, he had letters, said to have been afterward
identified as genuine.   According to his story,
he had been carried away from the Temple and
another child had been substituted in his place;
but this child having died, a second substitute, a
deaf mute, was put in the secret hiding place in
the garret of the Temple tower, which he described accurately.   Being taken in charge by
Barras, a member of the Committee of Public
Safety, who had overthrown the Terrorist Robes-
pierre, he said that he had been held as a hostage
that the revolutionists might bring Louis XVIII
to their feet.   Then had come the reign of Napoleon, who had kept him a prisoner many years,
part of the time in a donjon at Vincennes.   Later
he had been taken to the Vendee and then to
Italy, where Popes Pius VI and Pius VII had
protected him.

In support of this mysterious man's story, it
has been claimed that Empress Josephine, widow
of Napoleon, on the day before her death, told
Emperor Alexander of Russia that the lost
Dauphin was still alive and that Louis XVIII was
therefore an usurper.   'Tis said that when
Louis XVIII attempted to publicly "commemo-
rate the Dauphin's death" Pius VII forbade him.

According to the story of this man who claimed to be the lost Dauphin, he had lately left Italy and wandered on foot to Berlin, nearing which city a stranger had overtaken him on the road and told him that he would need a passport to enter. The pilgrim having no passport, the intruder pressed upon him one that had been made out in the name of another man, one Naundorff. So, as Naundorff, the alleged lost Dauphin entered the Prussian capital, where he set himself up in business as a watchmaker and let his story leak out. After a while the King of Prussia learned his secret and, it is said, obtained all of his documents. Holding these over the head of Louis XVIII, he exacted from that monarch treaty concessions disadvantageous to France.

Six years after entering Berlin Naundorff wrote to Louis XVI's daughter, the Duchesse D'Angouleme, claiming to be her lost brother. As a result he became the victim of persecutions said to have been inspired by the French King's secret agents. He was accused of arson and counterfeiting, but made his way to Paris, where he was identified as the rightful Louis XVII by Doctor de Caro, physician of his alleged sister, the Duchesse D'Angouleme; also by her dentist, by Mme. de Rambaud, once femme-de-chambre of the little Dauphin, and by others who had access to the palace at the time of Louis XVI. His story was accepted also by Jules Favre, the noted French statesman, who became his attorney and confidante.

Later Naundorff settled in Holland, where a military invention gave him means and where it is said the Dutch King accepted his claims. He died at Delft in 1845, his last words being a mumbled recitation of events concerning the prison of the Temple and the guillotine. During his autopsy the vaccination marks, a lip scar, a pigeon-shaped mole and other marks that had distinguished the lost Dauphin were said to have been found upon his body. His tomb at Delft bears this inscription:

"Charles Louis de Bourbon, Duc de Normandie. Born at the Chateau of Versailles on 27th March, 1785. Son of his late Majesty Louis XVI, King of France, and of Her Imperial and Royal Highness Marie Antoinette, Archduchess of Austria, Queen of France; both of them deceased at Paris. Died on August 10, 1845, at Delft."

King Louis Philippe, who, during the greater part of his reign, strove to disprove the claims of Naundorff, protested to William of Holland, asking him to obliterate this inscription. The Dutch ruler offered to comply only upon condition that the French Government would furnish evidence that the words upon the Delft tomb were false. Queen Wilhelmina of Holland lately had the tomb repaired and the inscription remains. In recent years the great-grandsons of the mysterious Naundorff have entered suit for recognition as the heirs of the vanished Louis and a Senate commission appointed to examine into their claim some time ago decided in their favor, although the Senate neither rejected nor accepted the report.

So Naundorff still remains a mystery. If he was not the lost Louis XVII, who was he? None of the hundreds of secret agents that have worked upon the case was ever able to identify him as any other personage.

But there were others who disputed this enigma's claim to identity as the rightful Louis XVII; and the mysterious story of one of these we will recount in the chapter which follows.

The Strange Story of Eleazar Williams

"Who are these that call themselves my father and my mother? Instinct tells me that I am not flesh of their flesh, or bone of their bone."

This suspicion morbidly haunted a strange, dreamy lad who, early in the past century, ended a hiatus and came back to normal senses after a hazy period of mental weakness. In his case, due to extreme youth, mental recovery did not restore memory of events happening before his lapse.

All that he knew was that he had suffered excruciating pain, which, others said, had resulted from a severe fall. It was further alleged that before this accident he had been weak-minded; that the persons with whom he now found himself were his father and his mother—these crude personages against whom his heart cried.

During the remainder of his years he searched for his identity. According to the best evidence that he could gather he had been brought to Northern New York by the Indian squaw and half-breed farmer claiming to be his parents. They gave him the name Eleazar Williams, and as such he was known throughout the remainder of his life, although there were some who later offered him the homage due to a prince, a king, a royal martyr who had been cheated of his throne.

Eleazar grew to manhood among the Indians and adventurers of our Canadian frontier. A giant in stature and strength, possessed of a fearless heart he naturally entered the War of 1812 and did brave service for the American cause, being severely wounded at Plattsburg.

His insistent claims that he was not the offspring of his alleged parents led to an investigation. Physicians who examined him proved to their satisfaction that he was not of Indian blood. Pressed with inquiries, his reputed mother once confessed that he was not her child.

Soon after this there entered upon the scene a witness who was to start rolling a ball of evidence soon to grow to great size and start the tongues of two continents wagging. This was Skenondouh, an Indian of the frontier. Skenondouh took oath that two French noblemen had appeared upon Lake George in 1795 with a feeble-minded lad of about ten. These great men turned their half-witted charge over to the Williamses who thenceforth were in no want for money. Goodly sums came to them regularly from somewhere. And it was doubtless to escape the curiosity of their neighbors that Eleazar's foster-parents had moved from their former home. Investigation further showed that the mother of Eleazar's foster-father, Thomas Williams, had experienced an adventurous career of her own. From the comfortable parsonage of her father, the Rev. John Williams, of Deerfield, Mass., she had been captured by Indians and carried to Canada where she forgot the English language, joined the Catholic Church, adopted Indian customs and habits and married an Indian, John de Rogers.

Eleazar Williams was sent to school at Long
Meadow, Mass., and after the war joined the
Episcopal Church, becoming a missionary among
the Oneida Indians.   In 1826 he was ordained
Missionary Presbyter and the rest of his life he
ministered to the Indian brother in New York
and Wisconsin.

In 1854 the Prince de Joinville, heir to the
throne of Louis Philippe, landed in America and
went to Green Bay, Wis., to hold an important,
secret interview with Rev. Eleazar Williams.
Why did this great prince seek out the humble
missionary?

According to Eleazar Williams the Prince de
Joinville offered him handsome bribes if he would
agree to renounce all right and title to the throne
of France.   Williams refused the offer although
preferring to continue his missionary work until
his death.   He claimed to have known that he
was none other than the "lost Louis XVII" of
France, and to have let the Prince de Joinville
know that he possessed this knowledge.

The Rev. Eleazar Williams had never been
known to utter an untruth.   He was as God-fear-
ing a man as ever wore the cloth.   Why should he
invent such a story when he did not take advantage of the notoriety that naturally resulted from
it?   Why should the Prince de Joinville search

him out in the wilderness? Why did that Prince come to America?

Eleazar Williams died in Hogansburg, N. Y., August 28, 1858, aged about seventy-two years. Many men who conversed with him were impressed by his resemblance to Louis XVI. Our libraries contain considerable literature supporting the theory that he was that unhappy monarch's lost son and the rightful heir to the French throne. If not, who was he?

Who Was "Pamela?"

There was high glee in the nursery of the Palais Royale, home of the Duc de Chartres, that near kinsman of the King, who later became the Duc d'Orleans. A beautiful child, a vision of loveliness and grace, a golden-haired, blue-eyed, mischievous, sprightly girl had been brought from England to be the playmate of the palace's royal youngsters. Her name was Pamela.

Who was she? Why had she been brought hither? At court nobles and royal personages questioned one another and shook their powdered heads suspiciously, but did not learn the secret of Pamela.

Pamela was born to be loved. The royal children of the household of Chartres, their governess, Mme. de Genlis, his grace the Duc,

princes, princesses and even their majesties
themselves, loved her from the first. She was
one of the loveliest creatures ever known to man.
And her loveliness increased as she reached
maturity. When sixteen she was described as
"a creature born to win all hearts. There was
never a girl more fascinating. She is beautiful,
accomplished," this worshiper continued, "and
the possessor of a heart which would make her a
treasure to any man who might gain her."

She became the toast of France, the favorite
model of its artists, the chief inspiration of its
poets. Many duels were fought on her account.

But who was she?

No one cared, save women who were jealous
of her charms, and their wagging tongues found
few listeners. There was not a princeling in all
France who would not have wed her, if he could.
But to all their race she said, "No." Her indif-
ference broke many a heart.

Yet a young Lochinvar was to come out of the
West and win Pamela. It was at the opera, in
Paris, while she sat in the box of the Duc de
Chartres, one night upon the eve of the French
Revolution, that the Irish Lord Edward Fitz
Gerald, son of the Duke of Leinster, first feasted
eyes on this charming belle. He was handsome,
brave and young—still in his twenties. It was a

case of mutual love at first sight. And despite
the opposition of Pamela's devoted governess,
now her duenna, Mme. de Genlis, the young
couple were wedded at Tournay the following
December.

Then Britain joined with France in asking who
might be this ward of the Duc de Chartres—now
become daughter-in-law of the Duke of Leinster?

In the marriage contract, still preserved at
Tournay, the bride was described as "Stephanie
Caroline Anne Simms, known as 'Pamela,' native
of London, daughter of William Berkeley and of
Mary Simms."

In later years her devoted Mme. de Genlis
maintained that her fair charge had been the
daughter not of William Berkeley, but of one
Seymour, an Englishman of good family, who had
run off to Newfoundland with Mary Simms, a
Hampshire girl of humble birth, on whose account
he had suffered disownment after their marriage,
and who had soon died, leaving her to work for
her living. But her poverty had been relieved
by a gentleman of the Duc de Chartres' household, who had come to England in search for a
playmate for his Grace's children. According to
Mme. de Genlis' story Pamela had been bought
from Mary Simms, as an apprentice, for twenty-
five guineas, this legal precaution being taken

to prevent the mother's laying future claim to her.

A third version of Pamela's parentage was, however, given in the marriage record printed in the Masonic Magazine the month after her wedding. This describes the contracting couple as "The Hon. Lord Edward Fitz Gerald, Knight of the Shire for County Kildare," and "Mme. Pamela Capet, daughter of his royal Highness, the ci-devant Duke of Orleans." According to this record the Duc d'Orleans (who, during the French Revolution, dubbed himself "Philippe Egalite" and who was brought to the guillotine by the Terrorists) was Pamela's father as well as her protector.

A fourth clue was given by Moore in his "Life of Lord Edward Fitz Gerald." It states that "Pamela was the adopted, or, as it may be said without scruple, the actual daughter of Mme. de Genlis by the Duc d'Orleans."

Which story was true?

"Life seems to me more like a beautiful dream than reality. We are so happy that I sometimes ask myself fearfully, will it, can it, last?" wrote Pamela to Mme. de Genlis after she had taken up her abode with her husband upon his estate in Ireland.

Coming events had forecast their shadows in

Pamela's fears.   Lord Edward's ambition led him
into the vortex of Irish politics.   He became the
ruling spirit of the Society of United Irishmen.
He played the same fatal card that Sir Roger
Casement was to play during the bloody European
war, a century later.   Crossing the channel, he
arranged for a French invasion of Ireland, but
was betrayed.   With a price of £1,000 upon his
head, he went into hiding, contriving now and
then to steal into Pamela's lodgings and spend a
happy hour with her.   But the night after he had
returned from one of these visits with her his
hiding place was surrounded.   Dagger in hand,
he flung himself upon his captors, but was
overpowered.

Pamela sold all of her bridal presents and with
the money tried to bribe his jailers.   Vainly she
begged to be allowed to share his captivity.   But
she was ordered to leave Ireland immediately,
and but a few days after her tearful departure
Lord Edward died, not at the hand of the executioner, but from a wound inflicted by one of his
captors.   She could not return to the Duc
d'Orleans, as that royal gentleman had by now
lost his head by the guillotine.   After numerous
wanderings, and to save herself from poverty in
later years, she married one Pitcairn, in Hamburg, but he left her in want, which she endured

7

until Britain relented and allowed her the money
due from her beloved Lord Edward.   This
enabled her to spend her declining days in comfort in Paris, where, just before her death, at the
age of fifty-seven, she was described as having
been "still admired and sought after; brilliant
in society, spirituelle and remarkable for liveli-
ness of fancy and playfulness of imagination."

Tourists who visit the famous cemetery of
Montmartre come upon a modest tombstone,
flanked by monuments erected to the memory
of personages whose pedigrees are given at great
length.   This simple stone bears not a date, only
the one word:

"PAMELA."

Tourists ask, "Who was she?"
And so does the world.
No one knows.

The Riddle of James Ord

"If you had your rights in England, James,
you would be somebody very great.   It would
make you miserable to know more.   God forgive
those who have wronged you, lad!"

No greater satisfaction than this would James
Ord ever give to his nephew and namesake, the
riddle of whose identity gnawed at his soul during fourscore years and more.

About the time when our seat of government was being moved to the banks of the Potomac, this man and boy had come from Europe to seek their fortunes in the new Federal City. James, the elder, became a master mechanic at the Washington Navy Yard, where he was known as Captain Ord. He related startling tales of his adventures under foreign skies and retailed many choice bits of gossip concerning the royal families of Europe.

The boy, James Ord, was entered at Georgetown College. A plentiful supply of money, out of all proportion to his uncle James' wages and apparent means, was regularly appropriated for his education and maintenance. Throughout his college days the youth was given to spells of melancholy brooding over the uncertainty of his identity. Not until Captain Ord faced death did he relax his determination to keep the secret, but before he could more than gasp—"James, lad, I've something important to tell you. Your father was—" the death rattle prevented further articulation.

"To my beloved nephew, James Ord," the old man's property was devised in a will still on file at Washington. But funds far greater than the possible yield of this meager estate continued to support the lonely boy. He weighed heavily

upon the conscience of some powerful personage,
who, from across the sea, continued to watch
him. Who was it? Even before leaving college,
young Ord determined to dedicate his life to a
search for his antecedents. This quest resulted
in some startling revelations.

The record of "Captain" Ord was carefully inves-
tigated, and it was discovered that he had never
held officer's rank. While but a humble sailor
in the British Navy, he had been discharged in
1779. Seven years later he had enjoyed a sudden
change of fortune. Through some influence at
the British court, he had been given a fat berth
at Balboa as Dockyard Inspector, under the commission of the King of Spain. James further
discovered that his own birth had occurred in
England immediately prior to his uncle's departure for Spain.

That his mysterious patron across the water
continued to fear him, was further evidenced to
James during the War of 1812, when, through
clever importunities, certain persons, later learned
to have been British spies, enticed him to enlist
in the American army. And only after it was
too late did the youth realize having committed
technical treason to the land of his birth, an
act that invalidated any possible claim to British
title or estates.

After the War of 1812 James Ord practiced law in New York, and married. Then came the call of the land of gold. He crossed the continent, and fortune smiled upon him. Having amassed great wealth, he attained distinction on the bench. Later he returned to Washington and built for himself a handsome home on Pennsylvania avenue. Then he removed to Omaha, where he died, at the age of ninety-seven.

During his eighty years of ransacking through musty records, Judge Ord came upon many bits of evidence other than those directly concerning the movements of his uncle. Not until he was forty-eight, did he gain possession of his uncle's confidential papers. Among these was a letter from one who revealed himself as a priest, but whose name was not given. It came from Europe, and asked:

"Is the child alive?"

At this time there still lived in Washington Captain Ord's confessor and confidant, Father Matthews, of St. Patrick's Church, an octogenarian. A sworn statement from this prelate is alleged to have quoted the Navy Yard master mechanic as having once confessed "that the child called James Ord and his nephew was not his nephew, but of royal parentage, the son of one of the royal families of Europe."

"Your father was one of the sons of King George III," the aged priest is said to have later confided to Judge Ord. "This was as far as your foster uncle would venture. But he admitted to me once that his promotion to the Spanish service had been obtained by a personage none other than the Prince of Wales himself. And actual negotiations were carried on by an uncle of Maria Anne Smythe Fitzherbert, wife of George IV."

Judge Ord thereafter firmly believed that his parents were George IV and this Catholic widow, whom that fat prince married in 1785, before he became King. His own birth had occurred within the year following their secret marriage, and almost immediately afterward had come his abduction into Spain. Rumors that a child had been born to the morganatic union had persisted almost from the time when news of the Prince's marriage had leaked out. The baby was said to have been taken to the United States. James Ord wrote to Mrs. Fitzherbert a letter, which should have touched any mother's heart, and it was delivered to her in secret, through the connivance of Aaron Vail, our charge d'affaires at London. She never replied. Shortly afterward, upon her deathbed, she requested that a certain mysterious package of papers be consigned to a vault in Coutts' Bank, London, there to remain until long after her royal husband's death. Fearing that this secret packet contained something that would compromise him, George IV made many futile efforts to obtain it.

Judge Ord died, firmly believing that it contained proof of his royal parentage, but when opened, by order of King Edward, in 1905, it was found to contain nothing intimating that the morganatic wife of George IV had borne him a child.

The Remarkable Case of Kaspar Hauser

A mysterious personage was found leaning against a wall in the Bavarian city of Nuremberg in May, 1828. He was a youth of about eighteen, apparently an aristocrat. Blinded by the morning sun, he held his hands over his eyes. The police told him to move on, but he could not walk. They prodded him. He staggered and fell. Questioning him as to his identity, they found that he could not talk, so they carried him bodily to prison. It was evident that he was not an idiot. His face and demeanor bespoke inherent intelligence. Yet his inability to walk or talk was unfeigned. He was not deaf and his vocal organs were capable of reproducing any spoken word by repetition. The soles of his feet were convex, like those of an infant who has never walked. Every sound seemed to terrify him, as did the sight of the commonest objects. On hearing a bell ring he burst into paroxysms of weeping and the music of a street band caused him to swoon. Given a substantial meal, he turned from it with abhorrence and fell into convulsions. All that could tempt his appetite was hard bread and water. Some one sent him some toys to play with, but they caused him to cry with terror, until he caught sight of a wooden horse, which he snatched up with glee, clasping it in his arms and kissing it tenderly.

He was an enigma to the authorities. The only clue as to his identity was a letter found upon his person and purporting to have been written by a Bavarian laborer. It stated that the bearer had been found at the writer's door sixteen years before, and inclosed was a note alleged to have been written by the youth's mother. According to this communication his name was Kaspar; he had been born April 30, 1812; his father was a captain in the sixth Chevau-leger Regiment, at Nuremberg, and his mother was a poor girl unable to support him. There were grave suspicions that these letters had been written for purposes of deception, inasmuch as the youth showed many evidences of aristocratic lineage. He was evidently a child of noble blood whom some powerful personage had hidden away because his presence in his rightful station would have interfered with that person's reputation or ambition. He had evidently languished from infancy amid absolute darkness and silence, suffering imprisonment even more cruel than that of the celebrated Man of the Iron Mask. It was difficult to imagine any one so diabolically cruel as to deprive this child not only of light and sound, but of the power to walk.

One surprising discovery was made. At the sight of a pencil the speechless youth took it up and forthwith wrote, "Kaspar Hauser"—evidently a name given to him to disguise his real identity. He was unable to write anything else or to pronounce what he had written.

In Nuremberg dwelt a kindly savant, Prof. G. F. Daumer, who became interested in the mysterious youth, and took him to his home, hoping to develop his retarded mentality. With surprising rapidity Kaspar thereupon learned not only to walk and talk, but to read and write. Within a few months he was able to relate as much of his strange history as he could remember According to his story he had been confined all of his life in a dark cell, penetrated only by a man whose shadow alone he could see and who came daily to wash him, dress him and bring him his sustenance, always bread and water. His only friend had been a wooden horse, and his jailer, although never speaking a word to him, had for some mysterious reason expended a year's effort in silently teaching him to write the name, "Kaspar Hauser." Finally, one night his keeper had entered his cell, blindfolded him, placed in his hand the letter later found upon his person, taken him to Nuremberg, and left him leaning against the city wall. That was all he knew of his strange history.

Professor Daumer's house soon became the mecca of thousands of persons who flocked there to see the mysterious youth and hear his strange story. One day, within less than five months from the time when Kaspar was found leaning against the city wall, Daumer was terrified to hear his interesting protégé utter terrified cries for help, and, rushing into the room, found Kaspar writhing upon the floor. Blood gushed from a wound in his forehead, and when revived the lad said that a man with a blackened face had stolen into the room, stabbed him and fled. The police scoured the country for the assailant, but without avail, and it was now quite evident that the personage who had sought to hide Kaspar from the world had dreaded the notoriety which he was causing, and had sought to put him

out of the way before his identity might be
ferreted out.   About this time the case attracted
the attention of the very wealthy Lord Stanhope
of England, who adopted Kaspar and sent him
secretly to Ansbach that he might be hidden
safely from his enemies and be educated by the
celebrated Professor Fuhrmann.   After a few
years, his education having been completed,
Lord Stanhope arrived in Ansbach to take his
ward back to England, where, it was planned,
he should enjoy a life of ease, compensating him
for the hideous persecutions of which he had been
victim.

On the day before that set for this happy
departure for England, a stranger handed Kaspar
a note requesting him to appear at a certain place
and learn the secret of his origin.   Without confiding the circumstances to Lord Stanhope, the
young man proceeded to the place appointed.
Soon afterward he terrified his guardian by
staggering into his apartment with blood dripping
from a knife wound in his side.   Gasping the
words, "Palace—Uzen Monument—purse!" he
fell to the floor, dead. Acting upon this clue,
Lord Stanhope hastened to the Uzen Monument
in the palace grounds and there found a purse of
violet-colored silk, containing a slip of paper
on which had been scrawled:

"Kaspar Hauser, born April 30, 1812. Murdered December 14, 1833. Know by this that I come from the Bavarian frontier on the river. These are the initials of my name: M. L. B."

A price of five thousand florins was placed upon the head of Kaspar's assassin by Lord Stanhope, and for years the police strove to solve the mystery. But their efforts were futile.

Kaspar Hauser remains today, perhaps, the most baffling enigma that ever vexed the mind of man.

CHAPTER V

Diplomatic Mysteries

Count Mattioli

THAT he might dominate upper Italy and keep the Count of Turin under his thumb, Louis XIV yearned to acquire Casal. This stronghold was the capital of the marquisate of Montferrat, part of the dominion of Charles IV of Mantua. Charles was a frivolous and reckless young profligate who had so dissipated his funds in pleasures and festivals at Venice that he had had to pledge the revenues of his crown to money lenders for several years ahead. Speculating on the financial distress and frivolity of the young ruler, King Louis conceived the plan of buying Casal for ready money.

One of the dandies at the court of Mantua was the Count Hercules Mattioli, the scion of a distinguished house who had distinguished himself at college, and who, when scarcely past his twentieth year, had been made a professor at the University of Bologna. Under both Charles III and Charles IV of Mantua he had served as Secretary of State and the latter had appointed him a supernumerary senator. Louis XIV of France was now represented at Charles' court by an astute and enterprising ambassador, the Abbe d'Astrades. This shrewd diplomat detected the ambitious and intriguing character of Mattioli and entered with him into a conspiracy to acquire Casal for France. After Louis had penned with his own hand a letter to Mattioli, the latter came to Paris in person and there the deed transferring Casal was signed. Under its terms Charles of Mantua was to receive 300,000 francs and as a reward for his part in the negotiations Louis handed Mattioli one hundred double louis and a valuable diamond. Then Louis sent to Charles' court Baron de Asfeld as his envoy to exchange with Mattioli the ratification of the treaty, but by Mattioli's instigation he had been waylaid and turned over to the Spaniards. Mattioli had thus interrupted negotiations that he might receive another bribe from the French king. In other words, he had betrayed both his own monarch and Louis XIV.

Louis, who had already begun to prepare for the occupation of Casal, was furious, as was the Abbe d'Estrades. The latter conceived a most audacious project—to abduct Mattioli. He communicated the plan to Louis, who, although he would not hear of any public scandal sent to the

Abbe a dispatch authorizing him to lay violent hands on the Count "as soon as you believe that you can carry him off without the affair making any noise." Mattioli, the dispatch went on to say, was to be conducted to Pignerol, where "orders would be sent to receive him, and so to guard him that nobody would know where he was." And Louis added: "It is essential that no one should know what has become of this man."

Catinat, commander of the French army in Italy, was personally charged with the minister's abduction, and the Abbe proceeded to perfect the preliminaries. Pretending, when in Mattioli's presence, to know nothing of the double game that he had played, the Abbe gave him to understand that he had been ordered to remit to him the remainder of the sum which Louis had promised for Casal. A meeting for the purpose of handing over the money was arranged, and on that day the Abbe and Mattioli entered a carriage. It was to drive past a lonely stretch en route to the place of negotiation. Catinat, with a body of soldiers, here lay in wait. The trap was successfully sprung. Catinat wrote to one of his superiors:

"The plan has carried out without any violence and nobody knows this rascal's name, not even the officers who helped to arrest him."

A chronicler of the time stated:

"The secretary (Mattioli) was surrounded by ten or twelve horsemen, who kidnapped him, disguised him and conducted him to Pignerol."

For Louis' envoy to have thus entered Charles' kingdom and kidnapped the Secretary of State was a most daring violation of international law and the French monarch had every reason to cover it up. He had to keep the imprisonment absolutely secret, and it was quite as important for him to conceal the circumstances under which Mattioli had been arrested.

What actually became of Mattioli after his abduction has never been known. One story was that after being imprisoned for fifteen years at Pignerol the unhappy Count was transferred to the French prison on the Sainte Marguerite Islands and later sent to the Bastille, in Paris, where he died twenty-four years after his abduction.

The story is that while in prison he was treated with the deference due to the rank and station of a great personage, but that no one was ever allowed to speak to him; that when he was sent out into the prison court to take the air he was made to wear a black velvet mask so that no one would ever recognize him. Baron Heiss, captain in a regiment at Alsace, in 1770 published a monograph attempting to identify Mattioli as the "Man of the Iron Mask"* and a number of other authorities have since dilated upon that theory.

So far as definite history is concerned, Mattioli's whereabouts were not known from the time he was kidnapped and taken to Pignerol. What really became of him is a mystery which, in all probability, will never be solved.

Chevalier d'Eon

"Sir, he is a woman! By fighting her in this duel your Excellency will make himself a laughing stock at court!"

So the Count Guerchy, French Ambassador to the Court of St. James, declined to go forth at sunrise and meet, upon the field of honor, his predecessor, that creature of mystery. Charles Genevieve Louis Auguste Andre Timothee d'Eon de Beaumont—popularly known as the "Chevalier d'Eon."

Born at Tonnerre, France, in 1728, d'Eon early attracted attention by a weird talent for impersonating either sex with such success as to deceive intimate friends. Learning of the talent, Louis XV lost no time in putting it to use to serve the, purposes of court intrigue. So the young "Chevalier" became the French king's secret

---

*See page 75.

8

agent in diplomatic affairs. He (for convenience we will apply the masculine pronoun to d'Eon) became the most successful spy that ever pried into the secrets that hold kingdoms together and break them asunder.

Part of the time, at the courts of Europe, he was a dashing young officer, with sword on side, who challenged his brothers in arms at the least provocation, who danced and flirted with the court belles, and who had the confidence of his fellow courtiers. He fought in the army of France, enduring the hardships of a campaign as bravely as he undertook diplomatic missions entailing the gravest perils, and necessitating the most exciting hairbreadth escapes. Then he would drop out of sight and there would appear at court functions a delicately formed, charming creature who had all of the young beaux and old roues of court at her side, who broke hearts (and purses too), who was the gayest flirt that ever cast sheeps' eyes at the sterner sex. For a long time no one suspected that the dashing Chevalier d'Eon and this court coquette were one and the same. The successful playing of both the male and female rôles enabled King Louis' spy to pry into secret documents, intercept dispatches, overhear dark secrets of state, eavesdrop and peep and pry, make and mar men intrusted with

confidences upon which hinged the destiny of
kingdoms. It was the most dramatic feat of
espionage ever performed in all history. And
d'Eon never missed his cue or overplayed his part.
He outspied all other spies of history.

Upon the eve of the great Seven Years' War
France sought a diplomatist with sufficient genius
to effect an alliance with Russia. After veterans
of the service had failed Louis sent to the court of
the shrewd Empress Elizabeth, at Moscow, the
Chevalier d'Eon. Presently it became rumored
about the Russian court that the Empress had
employed a new maid of honor, who was daily at
her side and who seemed to hold a spell over Her
Majesty. The pretty, bright-eyed girl slyly
directed the conversation into channels which
allowed her to display a wondrous knowledge of
life at the courts of Europe and gradually she presented arguments setting forth the advantages of
an alliance between Russia and France. Thus
resulted the alignment of France, Russia and
Austria against Frederick the Great of Prussia
during the Seven Years' War. Throughout that
struggle d'Eon kept the allies together with such
skill that Louis commissioned him as Ambassador
to London, that he might use his wiles against the
British sovereign.

The Chevalier arrived at the Court of St.

James in the guise of a man, but he had not
been there long until he defied his king. So Louis
sent to London in d'Eon's stead, Count Guerchy,
with ambassadorial commission for himself and
letters of recall for the Chevalier. But d'Eon
refused to give up his post and during the quarrel
that followed he challenged the Count to the duel
which that noble refused to fight because warned
that his adversary was a woman. He had been
recognized by some argus-eyed courtier who had
met him while playing his feminine rôle at one
of the capitals of Europe.

This recognition proved to be d'Eon's undoing.
He was beginning to grow too passé for the dual
rôle. Into his once delicate complexion had come
character lines that made disguise difficult. It
was another of the many penalties of age.

Some inquisitive British courtier dared to
ask d'Eon whether he was really a woman and
the little Chevalier promptly seized the intruder
by the throat, choking him almost into insensi-
bility. But throughout England it was widely
believed that the late ambassador of France was
either a woman or of uncertain sex.

An ugly feud resulted from d'Eon's recall by
Louis. He had Guerchy indicted for attempting
to assassinate him with poison and Guerchy
promptly had him indicted for libel. The quarrel

resulted in the Count's favor and the Chevalier was exiled from France. After spending some years in England, where his sex remained a subject of dispute, he was permitted by his king to return to France upon condition that he would henceforth dress as a woman.

A strong argument in favor of his being a woman was the fact that he accepted these conditions and appeared during the remaining thirty-three years of his life in feminine garb, using the name "Mme. d'Eon." Finding his prestige at the French court to be lost, he returned to more friendly London, where he supported himself by giving fencing lessons until, during a bout, he received a mortal wound from which he died May 21, 1810, in the eighty-second year of his age.

A post-mortem examination of the body is alleged to have established the fact that d'Eon was a man. But whether his propensity for feminine garb was due to normal purpose or to some abnormality of mind remains unanswered.

Racznowicz

The rôle of the mysterious, chameleon-like "Chevalier d'Eon," has been successfully enacted in our own country and within our own generation. The only patent lack of parallel between the chevalier and this equally mysterious character who, in America, reproduced his feats of transformation, is that d'Eon was more generally supposed to be a man with marvelous skill as a woman impersonator, while his modern counterpart was more generally supposed to be a woman displaying equal genius as a masquerader in male attire.

This human enigma of our time we will refer to for convenience by the feminine pronoun. Answering the appeal of her oppressed countrymen, she left her humble home in the south of Russia, joined one of the revolutionary "bunds" and, although physically a frail creature, assumed the masculine rôle once played by Louise Michel, the "Joan of Arc of anarchy."

With only eighteen years to her credit and completely outfitted as a young student, she became a clerk in Petrograd and skilfully managed to develop an acquaintance with influential officials who had her appointed to the consular corps.

She was stationed at first in Mexico, then in New York; but in the year of our great World's Fair, at Chicago, we find her appearing in our Western metropolis as a young Russian gentleman in the honorable employ of His Imperial Majesty, the Czar. For the next thirteen years she was destined to play a most difficult part with a cleverness which dazed her superiors when her true story was finally told to the world.

By day she was the manly, plain-speaking "Monsieur Nicholi de Reylan," confidential secretary to Baron Schlippenbach, the Russian Consul. By night she was the petite, girlish "Mlle. Racznowicz," a fiery "underground worker" in the Russian bunds which, throughout our country, in the days preceding the late revolution at Petrograd, were secretly plotting for a representative government in the motherland.

But as "Mlle. Racznowicz," repository of the black secrets concerning the dynamite fund, she was no more trustworthy than when, next morning, as "M. de Reylan," she received the stenographic dictation of Baron Schleppenbach's confidential letters to the home government—letters outlining his campaign against the dreaded underground workers.

This remarkable creature would have continued her difficult rôle unmasked but for the ravages of tuberculosis, which drove her to Arizona, where she died in 1906.

Wonderment at the prolonged success of her masquerade is heightened by the fact that nature had given her the poorest possible equipment for her daring rôle. Her weight was not above one hundred pounds, her skin was fair and delicate;

her feet and hands tiny, even for a petite woman.

Racznowicz had the vices which in her day more than in present times were supposed to be more characteristic of men than of women. She would stand at a bar and drink and was an inveterate user of tobacco.

This strange and mysterious personage went through the ceremony of marriage with a woman, and by those who later believed her to have been a woman, the ceremony was supposed to have been undertaken for the purpose of heightening the illusion that she was a man.

So skilfully did she play her cards that her political loyalty became as puzzling as her sex, and it is still a question whether in later life her allegiance was on the side of the Czar or of the plotters against his throne.

Benjamin Bathurst

Benjamin Bathurst, born in London in 1784, was the son of Lord Bishop Bathurst, of Norwich, and a descendant of that famous Sir Benjamin Bathurst who was governor of the East India Company and treasurer to Princess Anne of Denmark.

At an early age Benjamin Bathurst entered the diplomatic service and gained promotion to the post of Secretary of Legation at Leghorn. In 1805 he married Phillida, daughter of Sir John Call, Bart. Early in 1809 he was sent on a secret embassy to the court of Emperor Francis of Austria, whose empire was then upon the verge of a very delicate crisis forced upon it by the ambitions of Napoleon. England at the time was urging Austria to declare war against the French Emperor, but the cabinet at Vienna was as yet undecided whether to enter again into the perils which it had endured in the Napoleonic Wars.

Affairs were at this tension when Benjamin Bathurst hurried to Vienna as Ambassador Extraordinary of the British King. Encouraged by the message brought by the young Ambassador, Austria sent its troops across the frontier and Napoleon was known to be greatly exasperated. Bathurst, while remaining in Vienna, let it be known that he feared Napoleon's wrath. While he still waited at the Austrian capital, there occurred, on July 6th, the famous battle of Wagram, culminating in the armistice which in October led to terms of peace highly favorable to Bonaparte. His mission now at an end, Bathurst started back to London. Hesitating which road to take, he selected that through Trieste, Malta and Berlin. When he started out he had with him his private secretary and valet, and the better to outwit French spies, masqueraded as "Herr Koch, traveling merchant." He carried with him pistols, both upon his person and in the back of his carriage.

About noon, November 25, 1809, the returning Ambassador arrived at Perlberg, about thirteen miles beyond Berlin on the road to Hamburg, and here he alighted at the White Swan Inn for refreshment. A woman who saw him eating at the inn noticed that he shivered as though stricken with a chill and that his hand trembled while he raised his cup of tea to his lips. He wore a pair of gray trousers, a gray-frogged short coat and a handsome sable greatcoat lined with violet velvet. His cap was also of sable fur and in his scarf was a valuable diamond pin. Finishing his meal, he crossed to the market place, told the commandant of the town that he was a traveler on his way to Hamburg and requested that he might be given a guard in the inn while he remained there. Laughing at his fears, the commandant allowed him two soldiers and noted that he was greatly agitated with fright. Returning to the White Swan, Bathurst countermanded previous orders given for fresh horses, explaining that he would not proceed on his journey until after nightfall, as it would be safer to travel while hidden by darkness. So at seven o'clock he dismissed his guard and ordered his horses to be ready at nine. After the carriage had driven up, he stood watching a servant place his portmanteau in the vehicle. Then he stepped around to the heads of the horses and dissolved into the night.

When Bathurst thus vanished, the hostler and postilion were adjusting the harness by the dim light of a horn lantern and the Ambassador's secretary was standing in the doorway of the inn paying the account to the landlord. Not until the landlord and secretary had advanced to the carriage and while the valet stood at the door of the vehicle, was it discovered that the Ambassador was missing. Shivering with the cold, they waited and sent back to the room which Bathurst had occupied. Then they called, but there was no answer. Without a word of warning, a cry of alarm or a sound of struggle, the diplomat had entered the black realm of mystery.

After the alarm had been given, soldiers scoured the entire country round. The river was dragged and every nook and cranny searched. Three weeks after the strange disappearance two peasant women seeking firewood found in the forest near the inn a pair of gray, mud-soiled trousers turned inside out. They contained two bullet holes, but showed no traces of blood. In one of the pockets was a half-finished letter afterward identified as

from Bathurst to his wife and stating that he was
afraid that he would never reach England—that
his ruin would be wrought by Count d'Entraigues,
a famous French spy. This letter also requested
Mrs. Bathurst not to remarry in the event of her
husband's failure to return. Heavy rewards for
the discovery of the Ambassador's body were
offered by the Bathurst family, the English Government and Prince Frederick of Prussia, but they
availed nothing.

Various theories as to the Ambassador's disappearance were put forward. One was that
he had been lost at sea; another that he had been
murdered by his valet. Count d'Entraigues, fear
for whom Bathurst had expressed in the unfinished
letter, was, with his wife, afterward cruelly murdered by an Italian servant. Before his death
the Count was heard to say that Bathurst was
murdered in the Fortress of Magdeburg. A
German newspaper stated that the envoy had
committed suicide during a fit of insanity and a
Hamburg paper, late in January, deepened the
mystery by announcing that he was "well in
mind and body," that his friends had "received
a letter from him dated December 13th, which,
therefore, must have been written after the date
of his supposed death."

As this statement was untrue, there was a

suspicion that it had been inserted for a purpose. Bathurst's fur coat was afterward found in the cellar of a peasant's hut behind some firewood and the peasant's wife declared that she had found it at the inn and had brought it home. Another witness averred that he had seen Bathurst on the night of his disappearance proceed down a narrow lane, in Perlberg, toward the house where the coat was found. According to a further statement by the peasant's wife, the stranger had called at her house at that time and had sent her to buy gunpowder. The commandant of Perlberg always maintained that the Ambassador had not fallen victim to French spies, but that, if murdered at all, he had been slain for his money.

In 1852 a house once occupied by one Mertens —who was a serving man at the White Swan at the time of Bathurst's disappearance forty-three years before—was torn down and a human skeleton was discovered under the threshold of the stable. It lay stretched out, face-upward and in the back of the skull was a fracture indicating a heavy blow. But investigation showed Mertens to have been a respected citizen. Inasmuch as a favorable peace with Austria had been concluded, Napoleon could not have been vitally interested in any papers which the Ambassador was likely to carry upon his person during his return from Vienna.

Bathurst's disappearance still remains the darkest mystery in the annals of diplomacy.

The Mystery of Kent Loomis

Early in 1904 the American Government ratified an important treaty with King Menelik of Abyssinia, who called himself also Emperor of Ethiopia and who boasted of being a descendant of that Queen of Sheba who is mentioned in the Scriptures.

The Assistant Secretary of State, F. B. Loomis, commissioned his brother, Kent J. Loomis, as his confidential representative, to bear the treaty to the dusky monarch at his capital, Addis Ababa. The mission was one entailing little responsibility and much interesting travel, and Kent Loomis, being the editor of a newspaper in Parkersburg, West Virginia, had the mental equipment to both enjoy and fulfill it. After delivering the treaty he expected to hunt big game in Abyssinia.

Stating that he would be gone two months, he bade his wife and child good-bye in their southern home, and on June 14th sailed for Cherbourg on the Kaiser William II. But before the ship reached its destination he was missed and no sooner had the cable flashed word of his disappearance than all sorts of puzzling rumors sprang up from various sources.

Investigation showed that Loomis had been

last seen an hour or two after midnight, June 19th,
when he had gone on deck following the usual
captain's dinner which had been given on the eve
of the vessel's arrival at its destination. Shortly
after that time the ship made a stop at Plymouth,
England, where one passenger was positive he saw
Mr. Loomis land with the crowd, in which he was
borne along in what was described as a sort of
dazed condition. But the Kaiser Wilhelm's
captain and head steward, who both had stood at
the gangway when the passengers alighted, were
equally as sure Uncle Sam's confidential messenger
did not leave the ship with the other passengers.
Finally, when the vessel reached Cherbourg,
whither he was booked, a vain search of all of the
cabins was made for the vanished passenger.

A promoter, William H. Ellis, who was Loomis'
cabinmate and traveling companion, and who
claimed to be a Cuban, stated, when questioned,
that the editor's absence from his berth had not
alarmed him after the vessel touched Plymouth,
late at night, since the young man had been up
very late the several previous nights.

Ellis continued on the journey to Abyssinia,
bearing the tin box containing the treaty, and a
week went by without the appearance of a single
clue to the mystery. Then followed reports that
the lost man had turned up alive at Paris, that he

had been found dead at Cherbourg, also that he had been placed in a sanitarium at Plymouth—there to be kept until he might recover from a fit of abstraction. This fit, according to the last-mentioned rumor, had seized him about two o'clock on the night of his disappearance, and while he was acting strangely in the company of a man and woman on deck.

All sorts of contradictory statements as to Loomis' fate continued until July 16th when—four weeks after his disappearance—a body identified as his was found washed up at Warren Point, some fifteen miles from Plymouth. Under his right ear was a circular wound which appeared to have been inflicted before death, and, based upon a post-mortem examination of the lungs, the verdict of the coroner's jury stated that death had been caused by a blow rather than by drowning. Against the theory that the young man had lost his balance and accidentally fallen overboard was advanced the argument that the sea on the night of his disappearance was unusually calm and that the rails of the two main decks of the Kaiser Wilhelm II were high.

The circumstances of Loomis' disappearance from the ship will probably remain a mystery of the sea until all watery graves yield up their uncanny secrets.

Death Had Been Caused by a Blow

CHAPTER VI

Mysteries of the Literary World

The Riddle of Shakespeare

THE world knows least him whom it knows best.

It is generally conceded that the super-man who wrote under the name William Shakespeare, Shakspeare, Shakepear or Shaxper was the greatest author whom the world ever produced. Little is known of him as a man, save that he was the third child of James Shakespeare, a glover; that his grandfathers were husbandmen; that when eighteen he married Anne Hathaway; that five years later he joined a troop of strolling players and went to London, where, in two years more, he was engaged in revising plays; that he became one of the chief actors of the best company in London; that later he worked as a playwright; that at thirty-two he was able to buy a home at Stratford, where, at forty-six, he finally retired and where, at fifty-two, he died.

All kinds of conflicting statements have been written concerning his private life. Some claim that he was the uneducated son of illiterate parents; that even his own daughters could neither read nor write. Others would have it that he was forced to leave home for deer-stealing in the park of Sir Thomas Lucy. Another story is that upon his arrival in London he lived upon tips given him for holding horses of rich patrons of the theater. According to still others, after his return to Stratford he became a petty tradesman, selling corn and malt and lending small sums of money. It is claimed that during the time when he was supposed to be writing his plays he lodged in the house of a humble hairdresser.

Yet, some of his biographers mention his having owned shares in two of the leading London theaters. No two accounts of his life agree. Every statement concerning him is qualified by clauses expressive of uncertainty.

Until sixty years ago, however, no one seems to have doubted that the great masterpieces published under his name were written by this man of mystery. Then there appeared from the pen of an American woman, Delia Bacon, an argument attempting to set forth proofs that Shakespeare could not have written these great works. Since then other writers have waged a propaganda purposed to deprive Shakespeare of the honors freely granted by three centuries of admirers. One of the most zealous of these was Ignatius Donnelly, once candidate for Vice-President of the United States. Another is Sir Edwin Durning Lawrence, Bart., who in recent years has circulated a million copies of articles attempting to deprive Shakespeare of the credit so long granted to him. According to Sir Edwin, the real Shakespeare was but a "drunken, illiterate clown" who "was totally unable to write a single letter of his own name and of whom we are told, if we understand what we are told, that he could not read a line of print."

While some of these propagandists claim that Marlowe was the real author of the Shakespeare plays, a vast majority credit them to Francis Bacon, the greatest English scholar and lawyer of his day. According to the theory of the pro-Baconites, Bacon, by writing "Richard II," greatly incensed Queen Elizabeth, who was reported to have said, "Seest thou not that I am Richard II?" Bacon, afraid to recall his own identity, thereafter—'tis claimed—hid himself behind the toga of the Stratford actor.

It must be admitted that the author of Shakespeare's plays displayed the most profound classical learning and a deep knowledge of law, as well as an intimate acquaintance with the details of royal etiquette and of court life. He must have been also an omniverous reader of history, who had mastered Latin, French, Italian and Spanish and who had devoured the world's literature, ancient and modern. To some who have sought the man Shakespeare in the chronicles of his time it seems inconceivable that a country lad of his parenthood and rearing could have acquired all of this knowledge, which, unquestionably, was at the finger ends of Lord Bacon

It is argued that Shakespeare's name never appeared upon any play until after he had retired to Stratford, and this has been seized upon as evidence of his having been sent there by Bacon that he might remain in obscurity while the great plays were being turned out under his signature—Stratford, then being farther from London, in time of travel, than Canada is today. Strangely enough, there are extant no samples of Shakespeare's writing except several alleged signatures, no two of which are very similar, nor is there in existence a single letter addressed to him save one asking for a loan of thirty pounds. And the only contemporary letters referring to him are unimportant missives pertaining to money. None of his alleged writings mention picturesque scenes associated with his life, such as Stratford, the Avon River, or the magnificent Warwickshire country, whereas these plays are replete with references to St. Alban's, Bacon's home. Bacon's

qualifications for writing Shakespeare's plays
have been summed up as follows: He was educated not only in English but in French, Latin,
Italian and German; he was the compiler of a
book of fifteen hundred and sixty axioms and
phrases selected from the greatest authors and
works of all times.   Because literary geniuses
were frowned upon in England during his generation, he spent several years in Paris where the
literati were in high favor at court.

The vexed question of the authorship of Shakespeare's plays has been discussed in 20,000 separate
volumes.   In 1916 Judge Richard S. Tuthill, of
the Chicago Circuit Court, in an injunction suit
rendered a decision that "the name and character
of Shakespeare were used as a mask by Francis
Bacon to publish philosophical facts, stories and
statements contributing to the literary renaissance
in England, which has been the glory of the world."

Psalmanazar

Early in the eighteenth century the mysterious
behavior of a personage appearing at Landau,
France, led to his imprisonment as a spy.   Satisfying the authorities of his innocence, he went on
to Aix-la-Chapelle.   After serving there as waiter
at a café he enlisted in the army under the Duke
of Mecklenburg.   He would not have attracted

10

any particular attention had it not been for the
whimsical account which he gave of his life.
Traveling always under an assumed name, he
never would state just when he was born, nor
where, save that he was a native of the south of
France. According to his story, his parents were
Roman Catholics, his father's family "ancient and
decayed." He had been educated at a university
which he would not name. He had a marked
genius for languages and spoke Latin fluently.

Later investigation of his career proved that
he had masqueraded in the various rôles of a young
theological student of Irish extraction, a perse-
cuted Irish Catholic and a native of Japan, converted to Christianity, in which latter deceit he
was aided by a knowledge of the far East gained
from former Jesuit teachers

Proceeding further, he had passed himself off
as a Japanese of pagan faith, and at the various
places where he stopped he now ate raw meat,
roots and herbs, claiming this to be his native
diet. Later he devised a language of his own
which he pretended to be his native tongue, and
with great ingenuity he compiled a grammar and
invented symbols whose order was from right to
left, like Hebrew. There was no record of his
name until he entered the army of the Duke of
Mecklenburg. He then called himself Psalmana-

zar, which he afterward confessed to have been
suggested by the name of Shalmaneser, the
Assyrian prince mentioned in the second book of
Kings.

His next invention was an original form of
worship which he claimed to be Japanese. His
comrades in arms would find him facing the rising
and setting sun and chanting in his invented
tongue. He arrived with his regiment at Sluys in
1702 and his mysterious actions excited the interest of the Governor, who invited two churchmen
to examine him. One of these was William
Innes, chaplain of a Scotch regiment stopping at
Sluys. The examination took place in the Governor's presence, and although Psalmanazar conducted himself very skilfully, his imposture was detected by Innes, who entered with him into a secret
conspiracy to exploit him as a native of Formosa
abducted to Avignon, where he had been threatened with the inquisition by Jesuits, but whence
he had escaped to Germany. Innes then wrote
to Henry Compton, Bishop of London, interesting
him in Psalmanazar, and the bishop, accepting
the story without question, directed the chaplain
to bring his strange convert to London

Aided by the chaplain, Psalmanazar readily
gained his discharge from his regiment and in
1703 arrived in London, where he presented the

bishop with a translation of the Church of England Catechism into his native "Formosan." Delighting the bishops and clergy by the ease with which he discoursed to them in Latin, he soon found himself lionized in London, where the churchmen raised a fund for his maintenance and further education. But there happened to be in London at the time Father Foutenay, a Jesuit missionary to China, who challenged the alleged Formosan. Psalmanazar boldly met the missionary for a debate before the Royal Society and held his own so well that the secretary of the society invited the two disputants to a dinner, attended by the Earl of Pembroke and other men of note.

The Earl now became one of the patrons of Psalmanazar, who was "invited to every great table in the kingdom." Several wise savants suspected his imposture, but were unable to get the better of him. Invariably he parried their thrusts and left his listeners laughing at them. The Bishop of London paid for Psalmanazar's tuition at Oxford in the hope that he would be better able to teach the "Formosan" language to a group of missionaries to be sent to teach the interesting Formosans Christianity. Men and women striving for culture went into ecstasies upon hearing Psalmanazar lecture upon the alleged customs of Formosa. To give his discourses as much spice

as possible, he told his listeners that the religion
of his native land called for human sacrifice and
admitted that he thought it no sin to eat human
flesh, although such indulgence might be termed
a trifle unmannerly. He went so far as to present
Oxford with a manuscript volume describing the
coins of his alleged native land.

All of this while Psalmanazar was being coached
by Chaplain Innes, who engineered further impostures, such as an autobiography in Latin, dedi-
cated to the Bishop of London, which was translated into both French and German. Then Innes,
for his zeal in converting the fascinating Formosan
to Christianity, was made chaplain general of the
English forces in Portugal. Psalmanazar, now
left without a pilot, began to blunder in his lying
and soon found his patrons falling off. He then
had to commercialize his reputation by indorsing
counterfeit Formosan articles made in England.
Later he served successfully as a tutor, as clerk
to a Lancashire regiment in the Jacobite rebellion,
as a painter of fans and as a writer for a London
printer. Falling very ill, he was protected by a
clergyman who took up subscriptions for his benefit and under whose influence he became very
repentant, writing a full confession of his impostures to be published after his death. After that
he became a hack writer and for a time fell a slave

to the opium habit.   He was prolific with his pen, which is said to have produced salable material twelve hours daily.   He now mastered Hebrew, compiled a new edition of the Psalms, wrote on various doctrinal question, produced a history of printing, was the author of essays on biblical history and collaborated upon the "Universal History."

In later life he was a man of irreproachable reputation, described by Smollet as a rather pathetic figure "who, after having drudged half a century in the literary mill in all the simplicity and abstinence of an Asiatic, subsists upon the charity of a few booksellers."   Doctor Johnson, who delighted in his companionship in these waning years, expressed a desire that his own life should resemble Psalmanazar's in its "charity and devotion."

At his house in Ironmonger Row Psalmanazar died May 3, 1763, claiming at the time to be eighty-four years old.   After his death, according to his direction, there was published, for the benefit of his housekeeper, his "Memoirs of . . . Commonly Known as Psalmanazar."   It was a frank statement of the impostures and eager struggles of one whose identity still remains one of the riddles of history.

Who was "Junius?"

During a period of exactly three years there shone in the political firmament of England a mysterious luminary whose identity has been a subject of controversy for nearly a century and a half.

In a series of letters commencing in the London *Public Advertiser* on January 21, 1769, and ending on January 21, 1772, this unknown genius' vitriolic pen flayed both King George III and the Ministry of the Duke of Grafton with a brutal violence that was inspired by the most venomous hatred and scorn. The publisher of the *Public Advertiser*, Henry Sampson Woodfall, was ignorant of the identity of his clever correspondent, who unquestionably was a distinguished man of affairs, sharing many of the deepest secrets of state, who uttered his bitter invectives in a clever classic style superior to that of any political writer in the realm. All of these letters were signed "Junius," some of them "Philip Junius." In the same scholarly handwriting Woodfall at previous times had received similar communications signed, "Candor," "Nemesis," "Anti-Sejanus;" also "Lucius" and "Brutus." The pseudonym selected for the final series was believed to have been chosen to complete the name of the Roman patriot, Lucius Junius Brutus.

One by one the henchmen of the Prime Minister were selected as targets for this cruel satirist's vituperation, and many great lords and distinguished commoners trembled in their shoes, fearing that their turn would come next. Vainly did many politicians and their agents strive to get into personal communication with Junius and to track this literary enigma to his lair. But fortified within his hidden sanctum he continued to throw javelins into the government party leaders without hindrance, although not without fear, for in one of his communications he admits his consciousness of peril in the following words:

"I must be more cautious than ever. I am sure I should not survive a discovery three days. . . . Though you would fight, there are others who would assassinate. . . . I am the sole depository of my own secret, and it shall perish with me!"

Several editions of Junius' letters were printed in book form, one of the most notable of which, published by Woodfall, contained facsimiles of his handwriting as well as that of some of the prominent people accused of writing under his pseudonym.

More than forty personages were suspected of being Junius. Some of the most notable suspects were Edmund Burke, Lord Chesterfield, Gibbon,

Horace Walpole, Lord Ashburton and General Charles Lee, who was later the noted patriot officer of our Revolutionary War. Lee had a fault-finding disposition and an extremely caustic tongue, fond of abusing superior officers. An Englishman by birth, he had served with distinction in the French and Indian War, and at the time that the Junius letters were written he had just concluded several years of fruitless endeavor to obtain promotion from George III. He was engaged during this period in writing ironical epistles to the papers. It is an interesting fact that about the time the Junius letters ceased, he succeeded in gaining a promotion. Three hand-writing experts reported that they had proved to their satisfaction that Lee's and Junius' chirography were identical; but about a dozen experts were quite as emphatic in their support of other theories. Authorities who have devoted deep study to the identity of Junius now attach very little importance to the theory that Lee was the author of that genius' mysterious letters.

One theory accepted for a time by some authorities was that the nom de plume "Junius" was used by a committee of writers inimical to the ministry, and one of whose members invariably inscribed the communications drafted by the whole body.

"I know no man but Edmund Burke who is capable of writing these letters," said Dr. Samuel Johnson to Boswell. Yet in Parliament Burke had once made an impassioned address in which he said:

"How comes this Junius to have broken through the cobwebs of law and to range uncontrolled, unpunished, through the land? The myrmidons of the court are pursuing all their snares. When I read his attack upon the king my blood ran cold!"

The favorite theory has been that Junius was Philip Francis, a distinguished British politician. When confronted with the evidence of his authorship, he uttered denials so veiled that they were thought to be evasions. Being at the time a candidate for the Governor-Generalship of India, it was pointed out that Sir Philip did not dare to confess that he was Junius. His handwriting was very similar to that of the mysterious writer, and a copy of some verse which he had once addressed to a young lady was pronounced to be unquestionably in the same writing. Tierney, when asked if he believed Francis to have written the celebrated letters, said:

"I know no better reason for supposing the fellow to be Junius than that he was always confoundedly proud of something, and no one could ever guess what it could be."

Junius' identity was said to have been fath-
omed by Lord Lansdowne, who promised that he
would publish the facts.   But his death inter-
vened before he could do so.   Pitt, whom Junius
had championed in his writings, also claimed that
he knew absolutely who the hidden writer was,
but would go no further than to say that it was
not Sir Philip Francis, whose son was at the
time striving to prove his father's authorship.
Several persons actually confessed themselves
to be Junius, but all of these were soon dis-
credited.

Who this man of mystery was will probably
never be known.

The Vanishing of Editor Conant

A generation ago one of the most brilliant of
New York's coterie of editors was Samuel Stillman
Conant.   Scion of an intellectual family, he had
been reared in an atmosphere of learning.   His
paternal grandfather, a wealthy Vermont manufacturer, had been a presidential elector and had
founded an institution of learning.   His father
had been professor of Greek, Latin, German and
Hebrew in several colleges and had revised the
common English version of the Bible.   His
mother was editor of a magazine, as well as the
author of many books and possessed a mastery

of the Oriental tongues that proved of great value to her husband.

Naturally, such learned parents would select the higher education for their son. So, after having been graduated at Madison University, Samuel Stillman Conant was sent abroad to finish his training at the universities of Berlin, Heidelberg and Munich. Returning home, he became connected with various journals and eventually became editor of *Harper's Weekly*.

Following the example of his father, he selected for his wife a woman of profound education and brilliant intellect. She, too, had been educated abroad and had a genius for translating the foreign classics into English, for she was an accomplished linguist, speaking Spanish, German and French with fluency.

In January, 1885, this happy couple were in the autumn of their years. Their evenings were spent in the enjoyment of their books or in planning a future for their son, now in his early twenties. No family troubles or financial worries were known to interrupt Mr. Conant's slumbers. He was robust and strong. He had been editor of *Harper's Weekly* for sixteen years. He was now in his fifty-third year and his wife was forty-five.

The evening of Thursday, January 15, 1885,

Mr. Conant spent at the Authors' Club and appeared to be in the best of health. The next morning he left his Brooklyn home with the understanding that in the evening he and his son would go to Albany to spend a week-end with an editor whom Conant, Sr., wished to see. That was Friday, and after waiting for his magazine to go to press the editor bade a cordial good-night to his colleagues, adding that he would see them Monday or Tuesday.

When he failed to keep his appointment with his son that night his wife became alarmed. The fact that he had always been scrupulous about notifying her of his exact whereabouts added to her suspicion that some untoward fate had overtaken him.

No clue to the disappearance mystery was gathered until the following Wednesday when a man entered a place in Coney Island and borrowed five dollars on a watch and chain. Young Conant later identified the jewelry as his own and the description given of the man who had left it tallied very closely with the published pictures of the missing editor. The fact that the receipt given for the loan was signed "T. P. Stevens" caused considerable comment, inasmuch as "T. P." were young Conant's initials and "Stevens" was Mrs. Conant's maiden name. This clue was carefully followed up and the same stranger who had hypothecated the watch and chain appeared to have passed the previous night in a shelter hut upon the Coney Island beach. After obtaining the loan he had strayed into a store and chatted for an hour or two with the proprietor; then next day he had returned and had made himself so agreeable that the shopkeeper had persuaded him to stay to supper. After telling his host that he was Editor Conant, of *Harper's Weekly*, he had passed out into the night stating that he had to catch the seven o'clock train into Brooklyn.

Learning next day of Mr. Conant's disappearance the shopkeeper who had entertained him at supper wrote to Harper Brothers, but entrusted the mailing of the letter to a friend who after carrying it in his pocket for some time posted it too late to make its contents effective in the search for the vanished editor.

A week after Mr. Conant's alleged appearance at Coney Island a friend saw him leave a hotel on Fulton Street and asked him where he was going but received only the brusque reply:

"Don't you see, I'm going up the street!"

This meeting when reported at the office of Harper and Brothers initiated another search revealing a clue whereby the missing man was traced to a hotel in Long Island City, which he had left only an hour before the detectives arrived there in search for him. He was never seen or heard of again. Every crack and cranny of two hemispheres have since been ransacked for him without avail.

After his disappearance his wife continued to live for several years with their son in their home on Willow Street, Brooklyn, where she tried to keep herself busy with her writings. She compiled some excellent works on butterflies and a primer of the Spanish language which has become a standard work. A dozen years after the vanishing of her husband her life was further saddened by the death of her son. Deprived now of her last means of support, she became confidential secretary to the distinguished engineer, Rossiter W. Raymond, of Brooklyn.

After having endured for over fourteen years the pangs of uncertainty as to her husband's fate, she died in a Brooklyn hospital in April, 1899, and was buried from the home of General Horatio King.

The Identity of Marie Corelli

The quaint English town of Stratford-on-Avon has been the home of two literary enigmas. Of one of these the British "Who's Who" states that she is "of mingled Italian and Scotch (Highland) parentage and connections;" that she was "adopted in Venice by Charles Mackay, the well-known song writer and litterateur, and brought up during childhood in England;" that she was "afterwards brought up in France and educated in a convent. . . ."

So relates the authorized biography of Marie Corelli, author of "A Romance of Two Worlds," "Vendetta," "Thelma" and other popular novels. Fuller biographies state that she was the daughter of Count Corelli, an Italian.

On the present site of Wallack's Theater, New York, there used to stand a tobacco shop and factory, conducted by one Henry Cody. Ten years ago, when this industrious man died, certain newspaper reporters got a clue that he had possessed a deep secret, in search of which they are alleged to have ransacked his rooms and to have purloined his private correspondence. At any rate, they obtained evidence indicating that he was a brother of the genius who had long wielded her facile pen under the name Marie Corelli. But that novelist, when appealed to, denied the relationship. However, the search was continued, and led to an English schoolhouse at Elm Grove, Southsea, Hants, where was discovered a modest schoolmaster, Sidney Cody, Esq., brother of the late New York tobacconist. The school of this unobtrusive British teacher was found to bear the name "Corelli House."

The New York tobacconist, Henry Cody, had a friend, James Brier, whose intimacy with the Cody family extended a generation ago when he visited that humble family in England. At the time of the tobacconist's death Brier wrote to the former's brother, the schoolmaster, in England, and received in reply a letter which he has kept secret until the recent death of the mother of the little family—an old lady whose alleged loyalty to the daughter who, it is claimed, denied her, was such that she jealously guarded the family secret and willingly deprived herself of the honor of having given to the world a popular novelist.

According to James Brier's statement he visited the Cody family in London in 1877, bearing two letters of introduction. The home was that of a modest London mechanic. He met, among others, the sister of his New York friend, Miss Elinor Cody, and distinctly remembers his surprise at being introduced to a very interesting young woman, whom Miss Cody presented as "Marie Mackay, my sister." When, a few years later, he heard this name mentioned in connection with the authorship of a successful novel, he was

11

assured by his friend, Henry Cody of New York, that the novelist was his sister.

According to the story, as written by Sidney Cody ten years ago, his father (and that of Marie Corelli) was "as hard working a man as you could find in a long day's journey." But this poor artisan's family soon outgrew his purse. "So," related the schoolmaster, "I suppose in a time of distress, or crisis, our sister was adopted by Mrs. Mackay. . . . Thus her environment changed and she lived, as it were, in a literary atmosphere which fostered and developed a fine intelligence."

Speaking of his mother, he stated:

"She dotes on our famous sister. I believe the dear old soul would declare herself that she was not her daughter if Marie desired it. So we all long to let it rest. . . . I foolishly named my house after her, but I see where she was a sufferer from 'mauvais honte,' and you may be sure she was little pleased at my natural desire to honor her. But I have let the name stand, seeing that Corelli was an old Italian musician. The name was good enough for an educational establishment. Her nom de plume was, no doubt, borrowed from the same source, only poor old Corelli was not an Italian count or very probably he would not have been a musician."

Commenting upon the purloining of his dead

brother's "family secrets," Sidney Cody added: "You had better consign this letter to the flames or some day like fate may befall it and Marie Corelli may suffer in consequence."

But Marie Corelli has persistently repudiated all of these claims of relationship. Snobbishness is very seldom an accompaniment of literary genius. Her authorized biographies are all noticeably vague concerning her origin. They omit any statement as to date or place of her birth.

What is the truth as to her parentage and why should she conceal it?

"John Carter," the Prison Poet

Haggard faces and trembling knees,
    Eyes that shine with a weakling's hate.
Lips that mutter their blasphemies,
    Murderous hearts that darkly wait:
These are they who were men of late,
    Fit to hold a plough or a sword.
If a prayer this wall will penetrate
    Have pity on these, my comrades, Lord!"

Early in 1910 this verse, in a paper published by the prisoners of the St. Paul, Minn., penitentiary, attracted the attention of former District Judge John W. Willis of that city. Visiting the prison in search for the genius who could produce such lines, Mr. Willis found a man who although entered upon the register as twenty-four years old

appeared to be fully double that age.   He had a
hatchet face upon which a heavy black beard
could not be concealed by the keenest razor.   He
was of medium height and had jet black eyes.
His manner was refined and he possessed a hauteur
that marked him for a man of high birth.   He was
entered upon the prison books as "John Carter,"
but admitted that this was not his name.

According to the evidence which had been
brought out at his trial, Carter, while "beating"
his way from Winnipeg to St. Paul, in search for
employment, was thrown off a freight car by profane and angry train hands.   He had eaten
nothing for thirty-six hours and was desperate
from starvation.   After the train had disappeared
in the darkness he walked to the nearest railway
station, broke open the money drawer and took
twenty-four dollars.   An hour and a half later, so
swiftly did the community rise against him, he was
behind prison bars.

He was sentenced to ten years.

The young man had served nearly half his term
when Judge Willis took up his case.   Correspond-
ing with a London solicitor, whose name the
poet-convict gave to him, the lawyer found that
his client belonged to a good English family.
His father having died in an asylum for the
insane, and his mother being required to teach for

her livelihood, the youth had been taken by a
wealthy relative from whom he obtained an
excellent education developing marked gifts for
music and literature. But this rich relative died
while "Carter" was still very young, and had forgotten to remember the youth in his will. A
London banker took him into his office but John
did not like the confinement of the counting house,
and his family next sent him to Canada to learn
farming. Unable to find steady employment in
the Dominion he heard of an opening as member
of an orchestra in Minneapolis. He was on his
way there when overcome by hunger and the
temptation to steal the wherewithal to obtain
food and shelter.

Soon after his incarceration "Carter" began to
contribute his little classics to the prison paper
over the pen name "Anglicus." He early displayed his talent for music by playing upon the
chapel organ and his genius attracted the attention
of a well-known music teacher of St. Paul. His
verse soon went beyond his prison walls and was
accepted by some of our leading magazines. The
noted editor, Robert Underwood Johnson, became
interested in "Carter's" case, not only because of
the merit of his verses but because of the manly
tone in which the young man wrote of his plight
and his future. Mr. Johnson believed the writer

to be worth saving, and voluntarily wrote to the
Minnesota State Board of Pardons a letter asking
for a remission of his sentence.

Carter's "Ballade of Misery and Iron," from
which the above-quoted lines were taken, concluded with this masterful stanza:

> "Poets sing of life at the lees
>   In tender verses and delicate—
> Of tears and manifold agonies.
>   Little they know of what they prate.
> Out of this silence passionate
>   Sounds a deeper, a wilder chord.
> If song be heard through the narrow gate,
>   Have pity on these, my comrades, Lord!"

John Carter, the mysterious, was never known
to utter a whine or complaint. He repeated that
he had learned his lesson, that his release would
return him to the world a better and a wiser man.
Having proved himself a man of genius he was
put to work in the prison library.

The movement to give him a pardon and a
fresh start in life soon bore fruit. Editors joined
with Judge Willis and Mr. Johnson and the
pardons board was asked to grant the pardon on
"Carter's" alleged twenty-fourth birthday—April
17, 1910. The board granted the decree and on
this date the man of mystery walked forth to
freedom.

While waiting in the warden's office, just before

plunging once more into a world which he had not seen for nearly five years, Carter was asked to write some verse expressive of his sensations.

"I must have bars in front of me," demanded the poet, and the warden allowed him to return to the cell which had confined him so long. The door was shut and bolted at his request but presently he called for his release. Then he handed to the waiting reporters a poem of which the concluding stanza read:

> "Unreal it seems,
> Half ecstasy, half weariness and pain;
> For so I fear this haven of my dreams
> Shall vanish and the storm come back again."

Attempts were made to identify Carter with several men of letters who had mysteriously disappeared about the time of his arrest, but all of these attempts failed. The men who had helped him to obtain his pardon aided him also in hiding from the morbid public gaze after the penitentiary doors had closed upon him.

Then he "vanished like breath into the wind."

Who was he? Should we even ask the question?

Five Women of Mystery

CHAPTER VII

The Lady of the Haystack

IN 1776 a beautiful young woman with a striking countenance and irresistible charm stopped at Bourton, a village near Bristol, England, begging for tea and milk.

Although showing signs of superior breeding, she was in dire distress, at times speaking wildly, as if in the first stages of mental derangement. After wandering about the neighborhood all day in search of a resting place, she was overtaken by nightfall and lay down to sleep under a haystack where she remained for some days. Several ladies of the neighborhood, who found her, begged her to come to their houses, but she refused. Believing her to be insane, the townsfolk took her to St. Peter's Hospital, Bristol. But, being released from that institution, she hastened as fast as her shattered strength would allow to her haystack six miles away. Without bed or roof, she continued to live in this miserable shelter for a period of four years.

Although fed and clothed by her neighbors, she

would accept from them, by way of food, cnly
milk and tea, and the plainest clothing.   Given
anything luxurious or ornamental, she would
hang it on the bushes as unworthy of her attention.   Every morning she walked about the
village, conversing with the poor children, to
whom she gave various articles presented to her
for her own comfort.

"Trouble and misery dwell in houses," she
repeated to those who questioned her as to her
remarkable mode of life.   She spoke with a
slightly foreign accent, and a man who went to
her haystack to visit her for the purpose of
inquiring into her identity spoke to her in several
continental tongues without noticeable effect
until. he resorted to German.   Then she broke
into tears, being apparently very much affected
by the associations which that tongue conjured
up in her memory.

After the four years spent in her haystack, this
remarkable personage was removed to Britton,
a village of Gloucestershire, and there placed in a
private madhouse.   The celebrated Mrs. Hanna
Moore took up subscriptions for her expenses.
After some time her legs became contracted as a
result of her years of exposure, and she became
pitifully lame.   Thereafter she seldom arose from
her bed of straw, where she lay, quiet, stupid and

harmless, except when resisting efforts that were made to dress her or place her in a comfortable bed. She was finally removed, as incurable, to Guy's Hospital, Southwark, where Mrs. Hanna Moore continued to supply her wants until the time of her death, on December 18, 1801.

Detailed descriptions of "The Lady of the Haystack" were published in newspapers through the continent of Europe, but brought no response until nine years after her discovery near Bristol, when a mysterious anonymous pamphlet printed in French was circulated throughout Europe. It was entitled "The Stranger—A True History," and attempted to identify the Lady of the Haystack as a certain woman of mystery who had in recent years proved an enigma to the courts of Vienna and Versailles.

It appeared that some years previously the King of Spain had received a letter, purporting to be from Emperor Joseph II of Austria, asking him to take under his protection a young woman whose presence in Austria would cause great grief to his mother, the Dowager Empress, because she was a natural daughter of his late father, Francis I. The King of Spain replied asking for further particulars and his letter astounded Emperor Joseph, who had written no such request to the Spanish monarch. The forgery was then traced to a mysterious young woman living in great luxury at Bordeaux where she was known as Mlle. La Frulen. Being arrested, she caused a sensation throughout the courts of Europe by relating a strange story whose principal details were as follows:

As far back as she could remember, she had lived in a desolate house in the open country, in Bohemia, under the protection of two women and a priest, who had purposely prevented her learning to read or write. At various intervals she had been visited by a distinguished stranger, who had given her his portrait and also those of two women, one of whom he had told her was her mother. After some years the priest had announced her distinguished visitor's death and had sent her away to a convent in France, but while en route to that retreat she had escaped. After various wanderings in Europe she had been discovered by the Austrian Ambassador to Sweden and sent to Bordeaux, where she had been placed in charge of a woman of that city at whose house she was visited at various intervals by a strange man, who in a short time presented her with purses containing in all six thousand two hundred and fifty pounds sterling. Although this man had promised to continue these remittances from a very mysterious source, his visits suddenly ceased, and after a time she found herself overwhelmed with debt. Of the three portraits given to her by her protector, that of himself proved to be the likeness of the late Emperor Francis I. Another was that of the Empress, and the third, represented to be her mother, was that of a partly veiled woman.

According to the pamphleteer who related her strange history, Mlle. La Frulen remained where she was, as the Austrian Ambassador's prisoner for several months. Then he suddenly died and she was conducted by a young officer to Quievrang, a small town in France. Fifty louis were here placed in her hands and she was "abandoned to her destiny."

Whether she was the mysterious Lady of the Haystack or not—who, in fact, either of these enigmatical women was—remains one of the mysteries of the eighteenth century.

Theodosia Burr Alston

"Less than a fortnight ago your letter would have gladdened my soul. Now there is no joy, and life is a blank. My boy is gone—forever dead and gone!"

In these words, uttered in a letter to her father, Col. Aaron Burr, Mrs. Theodosia Alston, wife of the young Governor of South Carolina, bewailed the fate that had snatched away her only child, Aaron, a lad of eleven years. From his four years' exile, following his treason trial, Colonel Burr had but lately landed in New York, impatient to see his motherless daughter and sole offspring. Learning that she had collapsed as a result of her child's death, Burr sent his trusted friend, Timothy Green, to Charleston, with a letter, instructing Mrs. Alston to sail at once for New York. Prevented by law from leaving the state during his tenure, Governor Alston reluctantly consented to the arrangement. So the beautiful Theodosia, once the belle of New York town, was placed, bag and baggage, aboard the pilot boat "Patriot," which passed out over Charleston bar on December 30, 1812. Accompanying the melancholy lady were Mr. Green, her physician, several servants, several chests filled with costly feminine finery, and—some said—a recent portrait of herself, to be presented to her father as a Christmas gift.

During the first week of the new year Colonel Burr commenced his vigil at the New York harbor front. Day after day the dapper little man could be seen pacing the Battery, pausing now and then to scan the lower bay in search for the "Patriot." Days lengthened into weeks. Then, realizing the hopelessness of his vigil, he cried out in despair:

"She is dead! Thus is severed the last tie that binds me to my kind!"

Neither the "Patriot," nor the beautiful Theodosia, nor any of her fellow passengers were ever seen or heard of again. Thus befell the great tragic climax in the life of America's most dramatic figure, Aaron Burr. Shortly afterward his son-in-law, the brilliant young Governor of South Carolina, died—some said, of a broken heart.

Almost from the moment of the "Patriot's" disappearance there arose persistent rumors that she had been boarded by pirates and that Mrs. Alston had been borne away into captivity. After Colonel Burr's death two evil shore pirates were captured and brought to Norfolk, where, while in irons awaiting execution, they confessed that, with other "bankers," they had used false lights to lure the "Patriot" upon the rocks at Nag's Head, North Carolina, and that after blindfolding all of the passengers and crew, they had made them walk the plank. This evidence was later complicated by the deathbed confession of a grizzled sailor in Texas, who stated that he, with other members of the "Patriot's" crew, had mutinied, murdered the ship's officers and made all of the passengers walk the plank. Dramatic incidents of Mrs. Alston's last moments were dilated upon by this shameless rover of the sea, who described how she had been the last to go over the ship's side, and how her look of horror had haunted him for forty years.

A further complication of the mystery was yet to come. Shortly after the Civil War, Dr. W. G. Pool, of Elizabeth City, N. C., while staying at Nag's Head, was called to the hut of a poor woman, who, in gratitude for his treatment offered him his choice of many relics adorning her home. The physician selected an oil portrait of a handsome woman, which hung upon the wall, and which seemed strangely out of keeping with its surroundings. Pressed for its history, the old woman related that at about the time of the War of 1812, her husband had been one of the wreckers to board a pilot boat that came ashore at Nag's Head. To all who saw it, this craft had been a great mystery, for she had been abandoned and sent adrift with all of her sail set and her rudder lashed against her stern. Nowhere upon her was to be found blood or other evidence of violence or struggle. In the cabin the table was all set for a meal, which was evidently breakfast, for the beds had not yet been made up. Although chests and other baggage had been broken open, the booty had not been carried away, for the cabin floor was strewn with silk dresses, lace shawls and other articles of value, including the portrait, which she had just given to the physician.   Many who subsequently viewed this picture pronounced it a striking likeness to portraits of Theodosia Burr.

The mystery of Mrs. Alston's fate was made still deeper, only recently, when J. A. Elliott, a resident of Norfolk, Va., made a written statement concerning a corpse which, early in 1813, had washed up on the lonely beach of Cape Charles.   The body was that of a woman, showing evidences of unusual wealth and refinement. Before the stranger was buried, at the nearby farm of Mr. Elliott's uncle, three fingers were cut from the left hand, so that valuable rings thereon might be saved.   And it is related that this act of mutilation so preyed upon the mind of Mr. Elliott's aunt as to have a prenatal effect upon her daughter, born a few months later, with these very fingers missing.

Granting that all of these confessions and statements contain elements of truth, certain questions remain to further plague all wise heads that still strive to solve the riddle of Mrs. Alston's disappearance.   As that lady was in a position to guarantee a handsome ransom, and as she was a woman of great physical charm, why should her captors have doomed her to a death that could profit them nothing?   And, after killing all of the passengers, why would they have left valuable silks, laces and such articles aboard the "Patriot?" Why did they not scuttle that craft and thus hide all evidence of their crime? If the sea did swallow the "Patriot," what became of her? Why did no tell-tale wreckage ever wash up on any coast?

As the "Patriot" had been privateering in the war, some professed belief that the British had sunk her. But, if so, her women and children, at least, would probably have been rescued.

Some have suspected that the lost Theodosia occupies the grave of that woman of mystery, the famous "Female Stranger," of Alexandria, whose remarkable story we will next relate.

Alexandria's "Female Stranger"

TO THE MEMORY

OF A

FEMALE STRANGER

Whose Mortal Sufferings Terminated on the 4th day of October, 1816—Aged 23 years and 8 months—This stone is erected by her disconsolate husband in whose arms she breathed out her last sigh, and who, under God, did his utmost to soothe the cold, dull ear of death.

For a century this epitaph in St. Paul's church-yard, Alexandria, Va., has presented a Sphinx riddle to which no answer has ever been given.

Nor does there appear to be any likelihood that a solution will ever be found.

Our account of the mysterious and dramatic happenings to which this unknown woman's death came as a tragic denouement must commence upon the 25th day of July, in the year 1816, when the brig "Four Sons," bound from Halifax to the West Indies, diverted her course to enter the Potomac and anchor off Alexandria. She remained just long enough to lower a boat and send ashore a man and a sick woman. When the small boat pulled up at the wharf it was seen that the invalid had on a thick veil, which, in spite of the heat of that mid-summer day, she continued to wear while being carried through the streets to The Bunch of Grapes, the largest tavern in the city.

After engaging the best room that the hostelry afforded, the anxious husband—as he described himself—hurriedly sent for a physician, who was, however, before being admitted to the sickroom, called aside and pledged upon his honor not to reveal what he might see or learn concerning his patient. The physician's lips were sealed until his death, and the only information concerning his patient which could ever be obtained from him was that he had never seen her face.

She was veiled during each of his visits, for

ten weeks. Her alleged husband was the only nurse at the bedside day and night, through all of the enervating heat of August. As autumn approached, he became exhausted from loss of sleep, and two Virginia ladies, guests at the hotel, were permitted to administer to the sufferer, but only after they had taken solemn oath that they would never disclose what they might learn about the mysterious invalid.

When the stranger was seen to be dying, at midnight, Thursday, October 3d, the husband requested that only he should be left in the room; so the physician and two volunteer nurses withdrew.

A chill east wind rattled the sashes, a fine, cutting rain pattered against the window panes, and the two ladies, with the landlord's wife, shuddered as they waited outside the deathroom door. Finally, at dawn, the husband, with haggard face and swollen eyes, stepped out into the hall and announced that all was over.

Then, lest some one should see the hidden face in death, the supposed husband's own hands prepared the cold body for burial. He personally sealed the coffin lid. After attending the burial in St. Paul's churchyard, and ordering the monument with its puzzling inscription, he disappeared.

For a dozen successive years he returned on the
anniversary of his beloved one's death to put
fresh flowers upon her grave and see that its
grass was neatly trimmed. During these pil-
grimages of devotion he was ferried directly from
Washington and back, without stopping again at
the Alexandria tavern or speaking to any one met
upon the streets.

But, at the end of these dozen years, he seems
to have died, for his visits suddenly ceased and
the grave of his supposed wife became neglected.
The columns of its strange monument toppled,
and so remained until one spring morning, when a
distinguished-looking old gentleman and two
elderly women, handsomely gowned, suddenly
appeared in the churchyard to order the stone
repaired and the burial lot replanted. Under
pressure of questions from the sexton, these
unknown visitors reluctantly admitted that they
were relatives of the dead woman, and that her
husband had been a British officer; but when
questioned more closely, they hurriedly left the
cemetery.

Nor would the two Virginia ladies who nursed
the veiled woman at The Bunch of Grapes, ever
say a word as to what they saw or learned in the
sickroom, save that their patient was very beautiful and was of uncommonly high birth. Both

lived to ripe old age, and went to their graves with their lips still sealed upon the "female stranger's" secret.

That it was the lost Theodosia Burr Alston, daughter of Aaron Burr and wife of the Governor of South Carolina, who had come to this end, was one theory, according to which the alleged husband was a pirate, who had captured that distinguished lady.

Another story was that the "female stranger" was no other than Sarah Curran, the heartbroken fiancée of the Irish revolutionist, Robert Emmet, and that the "disconsolate husband" was Major Sturgeon, of the British navy, whom that unhappy lady was forced to marry after Emmet's death. But these theories were based on pure speculation and have gained little credence.

In addition to what we have quoted, these lines appear upon her epitaph:

> How loved, how honored once, avails thee not,
> To whom related, or by whom begot;
> A heap of dust alone remains of thee—
> 'Tis all thou art and all the proud shall be.

To whom gave all the prophets witness, that through His name, whosoever believeth on Him shall receive remission of sins.

The Veiled Murderess of Matteawan

"When I am dead, all will die with me. I have promised to be very still, to die without betraying anything."

A heavy blue veil hid the face of the prisoner at the bar. The prosecutor asked to have it lifted, but she would not consent and the judge did not insist. Her counsel announced that for this concealment there were good and sufficient reasons.

The mysterious defendant, either Canadian or English, had come to Troy, N. Y., in 1851, ostensibly to obtain a situation as teacher. Although she failed to apply for a position, she was always supplied with funds, with which she maintained a comfortable home. She introduced herself as "Mrs. Henrietta Robinson," and was reputed to be a widow.

It was discovered that she and one of the most influential bachelors of Troy were lovers. But in time there came to Mrs. Robinson's ears the news that he was about to marry the daughter of a well-known judge. Cast off, her funds running low, the jilted woman became obsessed by the turn of affairs. She discussed her disappointment even with chance passersby, to whom she proclaimed herself the lawful wife of her former cavalier. Upon the very day when his friends were discussing means of getting her out of town, a strange murder stirred Troy. A grocer and a young woman living with his family dropped dead after having been poisoned at dinner. It happened that the grocer's wife had been jealous of him and the other victim. It happened also that Mrs. Robinson, after having stopped at his shop to buy provisions at the time of the fatal meal, had accepted the invitation of the grocer to sit at the table and have a glass of beer. Although no motive was ever proved, she was charged with the murder and locked up in the Troy jail.

On the third morning of her trial the judge remarked:

"We have thus far proceeded with the prisoner masked. The singular spectacle is here presented of a person on trial for a high capital crime, whose face neither the court nor jury has ever seen. It is repugnant to my feelings to try a prisoner under these circumstances."

Rising in the dock, the defendant, with very stately air, replied:

"I am here, Your Honor, to undergo a most painful trial, not to be gazed at."

She was not again troubled to unmask. Her defense was insanity, but the jury, after having been out three hours, found her guilty of murder.

In passing sentence, the court seemed to be

impelled by a desire to add to the suffering which
fate had meted out to the mysterious defendant.

"To you life is lost, character gone, friends
are gone," were the grim man's mocking words.
"Everything is lost to you. Honor and virtue
are gone. Indeed, life to you is not worth
possessing!"

He ordered that she be hanged on August 3,
1855, but a week previous to that date the Governor commuted her sentence to life imprisonment. She was confined for more than eighteen
years in Sing Sing Penitentiary, then more than
seventeen years in Auburn State Hospital for the
Insane and finally for fifteen years in the Asylum
for the Criminal Insane at Matteawan. In all,
she served fifty-two years without revealing her
identity.

Fate, so cruel to her in other ways, was kind
in helping to hide her secret. Fire broke out in
Sing Sing and destroyed all record of her there.
From the time when the key of the Troy jail was
first turned upon her, she never wrote a letter or
signed her name. Some remembered that she
had helped to lighten the gloom of Sing Sing by
playing beautifully upon the chapel organ. In
her early prison days she had been an omnivorous
reader, but in later years she employed herself
almost entirely in making beautiful lace, which

she wore. For a very long period before her death her only visitor had been her attorney, who saw her about twice in a decade. It has been said that in one unguarded moment she claimed royal blood, and that in another she mentioned having a son who was a well-known officer in the British army. Her attorney was alleged to have admitted that for his services in her case he was well paid by influential personages, whose identities he refused to reveal.

The Black Angel fastened his seal upon her secret on May 14, 1905, a few days before which date she had said she was eighty-nine years old. The grave, unto which she bore her unlocked mystery, is a mound in the potter's field adjoining the somber walls of Matteawan. It is marked by only a pine stake bearing the number "88."

After her aged bones had been hidden away in the potter's field and while her cell was being prepared for another unfortunate, only one personal relic worthy of mention could be found among her effects. It was a scrap of paper hidden away in a secret pocket of her needle case and bearing this verse from Omar Khayyam:

> When first I saw this world of joy and pain,
> Assailed by doubt that ever will remain,
> I wondered what it meant to live, to die,
> The question oft I pondered, but in vain.

That "Henrietta Robinson" was an assumed name, its tragic bearer virtually admitted throughout the years of her incarceration.

"My father and mother are both dead; I have concealed my family name," she averred a day or two after her arrest.

She fulfilled her prophecy:

"When I am dead, all will die with me."

Dorothy Arnold

Christmas night, 1910, the newspapers received their first details of the most baffling disappearance mystery that has vexed the world since the kidnapping of Charley Ross. Thirteen days before, on December 12th, Dorothy Harriet Camille Arnold, daughter of Francis R. Arnold, a wealthy perfumery importer, at 11.30 A. M., left her mother at the family residence, 108 East Seventy-ninth Street, New York, announcing that she was about to visit the Fifth Avenue shops in search of a dress. Promising to call her mother on the telephone as soon as she found something to her taste, she walked from her home to Park and Tilford's store at Fifth Avenue and Fifty-ninth Street, where she purchased a pound of candy. Although she had from twenty to thirty dollars in her pocketbook, she had the confections charged. It was just about noon when she left

the candy shop.   Two hours later she entered
Brentano's, in Twenty-sixth Street, where she
bought a volume of humorous epigrams entitled
"An Engaged Girl's Sketches."   After emerging
from the book store, at 2.45 P. M., she met a young
woman friend, who congratulated her upon her
healthful appearance.   "I am feeling fine" said
Miss Arnold who, turning north, added: "I am
going to walk home through Central Park."
That was the last trace of Miss Arnold known to
her friends or relatives.

She was of a wealthy family, proud of its pedigree.   Her father traced his ancestry direct to
the Pilgrims of Plymouth Rock.   She was twenty-
six years old, about five feet four inches tall and
weighed one hundred and forty pounds; had a fair
complexion, dark brown hair and grayish-blue
eyes.   All told, she was a girl of striking appearance, the pink of delicacy, dignity and refinement.
She wore a tailor-made blue serge suit and black
velvet hat trimmed with two silk roses.   She carried a black fox muff.   She was strong and athletic,
extensively traveled and accustomed to going
about alone.   She had a very cultured voice,
whose accent was described as somewhat like
that of a French woman.   She was a Bryn Mawr
graduate with literary tastes.   Lately she had
written a love story entitled "Poinsettia Flames,"

also some verses, "Lotus Leaves," which she was endeavoring to have published.

She had very conventional tastes—was said to be the last woman in New York who would ever elect to visit the Bohemian cafés. She was not interested in the stage, in settlement work or any fads that would take her out of the paths frequented by conventional people. At the time of her disappearance she had out invitations for a tea in honor of sixty Bryn Mawr schoolmates. This function was to have been given five days after she vanished. A search of her room showed that she had left behind all of her jewelry of value and a large batch of personal letters. Everything indicated that her disappearance had not been premeditated. Had she planned to leave home without taking her parents into her confidence, she would probably have carried off her jewels in order to realize upon them. Had she planned suicide, she would not have purchased sweetmeats and humorous epigrams in the moments directly following a last farewell to her mother. Her clothing being of the finest quality and bearing the labels of the most exclusive modistes, it is inconceivable that her body could have been found without exciting notoriety —unless the discoverers of her remains wished to conceal her fate. Among her friends she was

known to be popular among many men but senti-
mentally inclined toward none, yet the private
letters found in her room disclosed one romance.
She was apparently about to become engaged to
a Pittsburgh bachelor.

At first the Arnold family concealed their
daughter's disappearance from the press, but realizing the value of newspaper aid in such an emergency, their attorneys at last gave out a bulletin
to the reporters. Thereafter, a series of conflicting statements and retractions served only to
deepen the mystery. There was issued the
statement that Mrs. Arnold was ensconced in a
winter resort awaiting news of her daughter, but
investigation showed that she and her son were
in Europe. It was stated that Miss Arnold had
no love affairs, but the reporters confronted the
family's attorney with alleged evidence that
she had been carrying on a clandestine correspondence with the Pittsburgh bachelor.

In spite of the general belief that Miss Arnold
was still alive, her family went into deep mourning for her. Evidence of their absolute ignorance
of her whereabouts is the fact that their personal
attorney traveled thousands of miles to interview
police and detective authorities and visit sani-
tariums and retreats of all kinds wherein the
young woman might be hidden. Virtually every

newspaper in the world has published her picture
and description. Both the Old World and the
New have been scoured for evidences of her fate.
Hundreds of thousands of circulars have been
sent to postmasters and police officials everywhere, and her picture was flashed upon the
screens of hundreds of photoplay houses. Her
parents have made several trips to Europe in
search of her and hundreds of thousands of
dollars have been spent in trying to answer the
riddle of her fate. It has baffled William J.
Flynn, head of the United States Secret Service;
William J. Burns, of the Burns Detective Agency;
Sir E. R. Henry, chief of Scotland Yard, and other
of the greatest detectives of the Old and New
Worlds.

CHAPTER VIII

Death or Escape?

Joan of Arc—Did She Thwart her Executioners?

FRANCE found herself in dire straits early in the fifteenth century. King Charles VI, surnamed "The Well-Beloved," had become deranged and Henry V of England had invaded the country, concluding a treaty which was to make him King of France upon the death of her mad king.

The rightful successor to the French throne, the Dauphin, Charles, was a youth of seventeen when this treaty was made. Two years later his royal father died. Then Henry of England came forward to usurp the French throne, and his legions became masters of the country north of the Loire, including Paris.

Now it happened that there dwelt in France at this perilous time a little peasant maid who could neither read nor write, but who had imbibed health from the great outdoors. She tended her father's sheep and rode his horses to and from the watering places. She developed alleged powers which in our day are called psychic or clairvoyant.

Going into a trance state, 'twas said, she saw visions and heard voices which told her that she was to be the virgin who, according to current prophecy, was to deliver France from its enemies. Her name was Joan or Jeanne, and that of her family either d'Arc or Darc. When seventeen she went to Chinon, where the Dauphin, Charles, held his court.

Charles, who in his subservience to the English had not had the courage to be crowned King when his father died, was persuaded to grant Joan of Arc's wish to lead his army. He ordered her a suit of armor, and when her visions told her of a consecrated sword which lay buried in a certain churchyard, that weapon is said to have been dug up and placed in her hands. Then, at the head of an army of 10,000 soldiers commanded by royal officers, all of whom regarded her as a saint, she threw herself upon the English, then besieging Orleans. Her presence at the head of the French army struck terror to the enemy, and within three months she had Charles crowned at Rheims. During the ceremony she, in her full armor, stood at his side.

Joan of Arc's promised work was now done. She begged to be allowed to go back to her native farm at Domremy, but Charles commanded her to remain with his armies. He feared that her

absence would turn the tide of his fortunes.
Joan thought otherwise. She told him that her
voices and visions gave her no further inspiration,
only the warning that if she fought another battle
she would be wounded and that her army would
be defeated. But she had to obey the King's
command. Leading her forces in an attack
upon Paris early the following winter, she saw the
first part of her prophecy fulfilled. She was
wounded, but recovered sufficiently to lead her
legions into Compiegne, then in the hands of the
English. She made an unsuccessful sortie and
the remainder of her prophecy came true, for her
army was defeated. Taken prisoner, she was
carried to Beauvais.

The divine power alleged to have protected
Joan of Arc up to this time now seemed to entirely
desert her. While attempting to escape her
prison by leaping from the dungeon wall she was
recaptured and taken to Rouen. The savants
then constituting the University of Paris obtained
from the King of England letters patent to have
her tried for witchcraft. The university gave a
unanimous verdict that her acts were diabolical,
meriting punishment by fire, and when the
sentence of death was read to her publicly by
the Bishop of Beauvais he gave her the alternative
of burning at the stake or submission to the

Church.   Joan chose the latter means of salvation,
but the bloodthirsty bishop repented the loss of
an opportunity to view torture.   He laid a trap
for Joan by placing man's apparel in her cell.
She put on the disguise in the hope of escape, and
the bishop seized upon her act as evidence of a
relapse into unbelief.

An immense pile of wood was placed in the
middle of the market place at Rouen.   Surrounding the pyre the English had a cordon of
soldiers and ecclesiastics drawn up at a distance
sufficiently far to prevent any of the populace
from gaining a good view of the martyr at the
stake.   According to the history which we
studied in school, the fair body of the sainted
Maid of Orleans was consumed in these flames and
her ashes were thrown into the Seine.

But many chroniclers say otherwise.   Indeed
among some authorities there has grown a belief
that the English frustrated the purpose of the
Bishop of Beauvais by placing the circle of soldiers
and churchmen at such a distance from the pyre
that an effigy or substitute might be burned and
Joan allowed to escape.   An eminent French
antiquarian, Gaston Saye, after a profound study
of all available records bearing upon the case,
concluded that another woman was substituted
at the stake for Joan.   His theory would account

for the French king's apparent ingratitude in
making no attempt to rescue Joan, although he
owed her his crown. An ancient chronicle of the
city of Metz states that a woman claiming to be
Joan of Arc appeared in Orleans eight years after
her supposed execution and was recognized by
her brothers, Jehan and Pierre, as their supposedly
dead sister. Thousands of people in Orleans
recognized her as the missing Maid of Orleans,
and the local authorities discontinued the annual
memorial service which had regularly been held for
the repose of her soul. Indeed, the records of the
Orleans treasury at that very time, show that two
hundred and ten livres were presented to Joan of
Arc during the month of July, 1439, "for the good
that she did to the said town during the siege of
1429." To those who have seen these records it
seems inconceivable that an imposter could have
thus deceived not only the thousands who knew
Joan's face intimately, but her own brothers as well.
There is also a record that Joan of Arc married
Robert des Armoises, a country gentleman, after
her reappearance, and a letter written to the Duke
of Orleans by her brother Pierre, thirteen years
after her alleged burning, speaks of her as still living. Indeed, court records dated 1476 contain the
testimony of a parish priest that in 1472, forty
years after her supposed execution, Joan of Arc's

family was entertaining her as their honored guest.

The question whether Joan of Arc was burned at or rescued from the stake is branded by Andrew Lang as "the most surprising and baffling of historical mysteries," and an old manuscript in the British Museum refers to the crisis of her picturesque career as follows:

"They burned her or another woman like her; on which point many persons are (and have been) of different opinions."

The Case of Marshal Ney

"I protest, before God and my country, against this sentence that has condemned me. I appeal from it to man, to posterity, to God!"

The doomed prisoner then turned to the firing squad, composed of sixty veterans of his own armies:

"My brave comrades, when I place my hand upon my heart, fire! See that you take sure aim at my heart!"

Raising his hand to his bosom, he thus gave the terrible signal. There was a ragged, nervous crackling of musketry, and Michel Ney, erstwhile Marshal of France, Duke of Elchingen, Prince of Moskva, dropped upon the ground, his face turned slightly to one side.

The dust beneath him became crimson with his

life blood. The soldiers marched away. And then a squad appeared with a litter, on which the corpse was borne to an adjacent hospital, there to be placed in a leaden coffin encased within a casket of oak. Early next morning it was taken to the cemetery and buried.

Such is history's account of the great hero's tragic ending. His crime had been loyalty to his old commander, Napoleon. Placed at the head of an army sent by Louis XVIII, to capture the fugitive from Elba, Ney had fallen upon his knees before his former Emperor and brought him, victorious, into Paris. Then had come the surrender to the Allies, Napoleon's exile to St. Helena, Ney's own flight, his capture in a friend's castle, his trial and condemnation; his execution on the 5th of December, 1815.

The day following the marshal's funeral, Philip Petrie, a sailor while holystoning the deck of a vessel bound from Bordeaux to Charleston, S. C., glanced up, and, recognizing a ruddy-faced individual, saluted respectfully.

"Who do you think I am?" asked the passenger.

"My old commander, Marshal Ney," said Petrie, very positively.

"Marshal Ney was executed two days ago in Paris," replied the stranger; and, during the remainder of the voyage, he remained in hiding.

A few weeks later several French immigrants, meeting a familiar figure upon the streets of Georgetown, S. C., cried out: "Mon Dieu, le Marechal Ney!" whereupon the personage thus addressed vanished.

It was about this time that a mysterious stranger, calling himself Peter Ney, appeared at Cheraw, S. C., and there engaged himself to teach the school at Brownsville, nearby. Glancing at a newspaper one morning in the schoolroom, he fell in a swoon, and school had to be dismissed. That night he was observed to be burning documents, decorations and badges. Next morning he was found in bed with his throat cut, the blade of his pocket knife being broken off in the wound, which, thanks to good nursing, healed. The newspaper, which caused the fainting fit, contained news of Napoleon's death. Later, when shown a paper, announcing the death of Napoleon's son, the schoolmaster suffered another paroxysm, and proceeded to burn more manuscripts.

One morning, while at Statesville, S. C., John Snyder and Frederick Barr, veterans of the Napoleonic wars, recognized the schoolmaster as the Field Marshal of France. Snyder went so far as to speak to the alleged Peter Ney, but received only black looks for his pains.

The schoolmaster, while upon his deathbed, in the early winter of 1846, was pressed by his physician to clear up the mystery of his identity.

"I am Marshal Ney, of France!" the Frenchman gasped with almost his dying breath. And, after his funeral, one of his intimate friends, Mrs. Mary C. Dalton, of Iredell County, N. C., revealed what she claimed to have been a confession made to her by "Peter" Ney shortly before his death. According to this story, the teacher was the great Marshal of France. Wellington had interceded and saved his life. The firing squad had been instructed to fire over his head, but not until he should give the signal by pressing his hand to his heart, by which action he burst a bag of red fluid secreted beneath his shirt. To insure the success of these deceptions, trusted men from his own army were selected to fill the firing squad. At the hospital, whither he had been brought upon the litter, he was that night disguised in ill-fitting clothes and started on his way to Bordeaux. There, posing as a servant carrying a valise, he embarked for Charleston.

History proves that Marshal Ney's trial and its preliminaries were conducted by secret methods. Members of the Assembly who voted for his execution, did so with the understanding from the King that the death sentence was to be commuted to life in exile.

Wishing to satisfy himself as to the mystery clinging to the Ney case, Louis Napoleon, after coming to the throne is said to have ordered the marshal's grave opened. When searched, the inner coffin is reported to have contained not a bone, not one relic of a human corpse.

Carolinians, who knew Schoolmaster Ney when shown portraits of the great Marshal of France, pronounced the likeness to have been precisely like that of their friend. Both the teacher and the marshal were ruddy of face. Each slept but five hours a night; each was a good fencer, a fearless horseman, a skilled mathematician and a clever performer upon the flute.

But, if Marshal Ney did escape to America, why did he not return to his beloved France after amnesty had been granted to all political exiles?

The Duke of Praslin

One morning in August, 1847, persons passing on the Rue Saint-Honore, Paris, were terrified to hear piercing screams issue from behind the walls surrounding the magnificent house of the Duke of Praslin.

His Grace, a personage of great prestige and power in the court of Louis Philippe, was the heir to vast wealth, and his beautiful, talented wife, was also possessed of a great fortune in her own right. They had been married nineteen years, and their union had been blessed by nine children.

Alarmed at those terrible shrieks of agony, the servants within the Duke's mansion traced them to their mistress' bedroom, which beautiful apartment was a reproduction of Marie Antoinette's bed-chamber at Versailles. Entering the room, they found the furniture upset, the bed curtains torn down and terrible splotches of blood everywhere. Crouching against a chair was the corpse of the Duchess, wearing only a nightgown stained with blood gushing from five wounds. Bloody finger marks were upon the wall on three sides of the great chambers, and upon several pieces of furniture were strands of her long hair, which also adhered to the handle of a bloody pistol found in the room.

Fleeing from the murder chamber in horror, the servants called the attachés of the household together in the great drawing-room of the mansion and were disputing how to announce the terrible news to the Duke, when he suddenly appeared in their midst, inquiring as to the cause of the commotion. When told what had happened, he at once sent for the police and a physician. Making his way into his wife's room, he then viewed the corpse and threw himself upon the empty bed, giving way to the agony of grief.

After the arrival of the police strange incidents began to develop. The Duke volunteered the information that he had discovered the murder before his servants had announced it to him; that, awakened by his wife's shrieks, he had rushed into the room, found her dead and had returned to his own bed-chamber, stunned by the horrible sight; that the pistol found in her room was his —in fact, that he had brought it into the room to defend her when he first heard her cries of agony. During their examination of the house, the police found in the Duke's apartment a dressing gown completely soaked with blood, also a hunting knife, poniard, and short sword, all containing bloodstains. It was found also that the Duke's hands were covered with scratches, that one of his arms had been bitten. In the fireplace of his room were a number of half-burnt papers, some of which proved to be letters received by him from his wife protesting against his interest in the governess of their children, Henriette Deluzy.

Many unburnt letters written by the Duchess to her husband threw light upon the Duke's relations with this unusually clever young woman. According to this evidence, and that given by others, Mlle. Deluzy had appealed more to the

Duke's intellectual side than had his wife; and although his interest in her had increased, their attachment had apparently been only platonic. She had a wide interest in politics and literature, while the Duchess had been of a brooding, introspective temperament. They had quarreled over the clever governess. In one letter complaining of the breach between them the Duchess had written to the Duke:

"I am dying of grief! For five long years I have spent all my nights in tears, in convulsions of sorrow. Often I have had to bite my pillow in order to stifle my sobs, my cries.

"I have lost not only my husband, but my children. I suffer the tortures of Tantalus. I am close to you all, and yet I am apart from you all!"

Finally the Duchess became so wrought up as to appeal to her father, the noted Marshal Sabatini, as a result of whose tactful intervention the Duke ordered the governess' dismissal but at the same time wrote his wife a note containing this one sentence: "By your act you have spoiled my life." It was directly after this that Paris, which had regarded the Duke and Duchess as an ideally happy couple, had been shocked by the news of her Grace's foul murder and the subsequent eccentric behavior of her husband.

When jealousy between husband and wife
results in murder, it is the jealous one who is
almost invariably the perpetrator of the crime.
Hence, in this case, had the Duke, rather than
the Duchess, been found murdered, there would
not have been any deep mystery concerning the
affair.   But what possible motive could the Duke
of Praslin have had in murdering his wife after
yielding to her demands for the dismissal of a
valued employee against whom she had cherished
an apparently groundless jealousy?

King Louis Philippe reluctantly consented to a
warrant for the Duke of Praslin, but before his
Grace could be taken to prison he swallowed a
large dose of poison, and the King ordered that
he be tried before the drug could take effect.
Hence, the jury, consisting of six of his fellow-
members of the House of Peers, was sent to his
bed-chamber, where the Lord Chancellor of France
proceeded with his interrogation.   After evading
a long list of questions asked him, the Duke
persistently repeated, "I am not guilty!" and
expired in agony.

Such was the account of his trial and its tragic
denouement publicly announced in Paris; but it
is still believed by a great number of Frenchmen
that Louis Philippe entered with the peers sent
to the Duke's bedside into a conspiracy to allow

that nobleman to escape and that he was smuggled out of the country in disguise, afterward enjoying a long exile in England, where he received his income from his eldest son, and later his grandson, until he died of old age.

As to Mlle. Deluzy, the market women of Paris threatened to lynch her. After she had been kept in prison for three months it was given out that she had gone to England, but, as a matter of fact, she remained for some time under an assumed name in France, whence she embarked to America to teach in one of our most celebrated private schools and later to marry a well-known literary and legal light of New York city. She and her husband moved to Massachusetts, where she became an intimate of Mrs. Harriet Beecher Stowe, and where she died in 1874, upon the eve of the publication of a book which came from her pen, but which contained not a line bearing upon the black mystery which the Duke and Duchess of Praslin left in their wake.

Wilkes Boot

"The body buried in Greenmount was not that of Booth," declared Basil Moxley, a pall-bearer at the alleged funeral of Lincoln's assassin, held in Baltimore.

"I do not believe that Booth was ever killed in

that barn," added Moxley, who for nearly a half century had been doorkeeper in Baltimore at the Holliday Street Theater and at Ford's Opera House. He was a trusted friend of the Booth family and a cyclopedia of information concerning the stage folk of his time

Many men have shared Moxley's doubt as to the most commonly accepted version of the capture, shooting and burial of Lincoln's murderer. According to history, the demented actor, after shooting the President, and after breaking his leg while making his escape, took refuge in Garrett's tobacco barn, near Bowling Green, Va. The barn was surrounded by twenty-eight veterans of the Sixteenth New York Cavalry, who, fearing to go in and capture one defiant man, set the building on fire and then shot Booth as he appeared to take aim at his pursuers.

The commonly accepted story of what next happened relates that Booth's body was sewed up in a saddle blanket and carried aboard the monitor "Montauk," where it was laid in the carpenter's bunk in the turret. After an autopsy in Washington, it was placed in a pine gun-box and secretly buried beneath the floor of a cell in the old Washington Penitentiary. After nearly four years had elapsed the great actor, Edwin Booth, persuaded President Andrew Johnson to allow the pine box bearing his brother's bones to be removed to Baltimore for secret burial in Greenmount Cemetery

Since the black tragedy of '65 there have been advanced more than fifty theories to the effect that Wilkes Booth escaped to enjoy life for a considerable time after his corpse was believed to have molded in its grave. General Eckert, who was Assistant Secretary of War when Lincoln was assassinated, and who later became president of the Western Union Telegraph Company, was quoted as having confessed to his nurse, on his deathbed, that with three other men he had taken the body of Booth out on Delaware Bay and thrown it into the water. A secret service man assigned to the assassination was quoted as stating that the identification of the corpse supposed to have been Booth's was never satisfactorily made. Such doubts and contradictions reiterated by men closely concerned in the search for the assassin led to the suspicion that greed for the seventy-five thousand dollars reward offered for Booth by the government resulted in the shooting of another man.

A few years ago Laura Ida Booth (Mrs. L. A. Howard), an actress, who has claimed to be the daughter of Wilkes Booth, announced that her father lived until 1903, when his long-troubled conscience led him to commit suicide at Enid, Okla. A Memphis attorney, Finis L. Bates, who knew the Enid suicide, and who believes him to have been Lincoln's assassin, has published a book in support of the theory. Some years ago Mr. Bates appealed to the National House of Representatives to definitely determine the identity of the embalmed corpse of the suicide, which, for four years, had been kept by an Enid undertaker. In his communication to Congress, Mr. Bates stated:

"I knew Booth as John D. Heley while living in 1872, and was associated with him as my client until the fall of 1877, when we separated in western Texas, he going to Leadville, Col., and I returning to Memphis. Booth left with me a small tintype for his future identification. This picture was taken some twelve years after the assassination of Lincoln and has been identified by Junius Brutus Booth, eldest nephew of John Wilkes Booth, as being the picture of his uncle. It has also been identified by the famous actor, the late Joseph Jefferson, and many others."

About a score of years after the Lincoln tragedy one Christopher C. Ritter, while lying very low in a hospital in Anderson, Ind., is alleged to have unburdened his conscience by confessing that after having been initiated into the Knights of the

Golden Circle by Booth, he had been pressed to take part in a kidnapping of President Lincoln, but that before the plan was carried out Booth killed the President. Accompanying the escaped assassin to Philadelphia, Ritter claimed that he sailed with him for South America, where Booth became "Enos," the famous actor of Latin-America

According to another story, Booth became an Episcopal clergyman and settled in a Georgia town, where he was visited by his brother, Edwin Booth. He continued to limp until death and failed also to disguise his love for liquor and his imperious temper. One story has it that the assassin spent the latter days of his life under the name of David E. George, and that he married a Kentucky widow; their child, a daughter, winning success upon the stage.

In New Orleans, Louisville, Denver, Albuquerque, San Francisco and Montreal the man who shot Lincoln was "located" during the generation following the Civil War. Improbable as the many theories as to his escape may seem, and after all of them have been sifted out and discarded, Wilkes Booth has nevertheless bequeathed to the world a mystery that has never been solved.

Where lie the bones of the man shot in the

Garrett barn, whose body was brought to Washington and dissected?

No one knows?

It is generally believed that the mound alleged to mark the assassin's grave in Greenmount Cemetery, Baltimore, covers no human remains. For fear of vandalism the Booth family very wisely hid the coffin which they buried.

"Morgan the Raider"

Another Civil War celebrity alleged to have entered the realm of the "living dead," was that daring American soldier, John Hunt Morgan, popularly known as "Morgan the Raider." History says that this fearless officer was killed while attempting to escape from his Union captors in 1864. Tradition says otherwise.

Morgan was born in Alabama and when a child was brought by his parents to Kentucky. In the Mexican War he fought with Zachary Taylor and in '61 offered his sword to the Confederate cause, first distinguishing himself at the head of a squadron of cavalry, in the Battle of Shiloh.

Morgan was not at all lacking in faith in himself. At the head of twelve hundred men he now began his career as a raider, and his first exploit was an invasion of Kentucky from eastern Tennessee.

It was his conviction that while he rode through his home state vast hordes of men would flock to his standard—that he would become the liberator of Kentucky. Defeating the Union troops at Tompkinsville, he uttered a fiery proclamation and began preparing for Bragg's invasion of that State.

True to his anticipations, many young men joined Morgan, and his force charged through Kentucky upon a career of plunder and destruction. Like a thief in the night he would descend upon the Union forces and take large numbers of them prisoners, and the next day he would be heard of burning bridges and destroying railway tracks, carrying off horses, raiding stores and terrifying the natives wherever he went. Louisville and Cincinnati trembled with fear that he would descend upon them. He planned to cross the Ohio River to pave the way for the capture of these two cities and to organize a counter-revolution against those pacifists known as the "Knights of the Golden Circle" or "Sons of Liberty." Then he crossed the Cumberland, sacked the town of Columbia, captured a Union force at Lebanon and burned the town. More and more men followed him as he proceeded toward the Ohio, and by the time he reached that river near Louisville he had a force of four thousand. Capturing two steamboats, he crossed the river,

plundered Corydon, Ind.; carried away three
hundred horses, exacted tribute from property
owners and sacked village after village. Indiana
and Ohio were both bitterly aroused and big
Union forces now put him to rout, but not
until after a retreat, during which he terrorized
many other towns, was he captured at New
Lisbon.

It was with a sense of great satisfaction that his
Union captors locked him in the Ohio Penitentiary
at Columbus, but after he had been there a few
months he and six of his men escaped. Now
followed a thrilling race between the dashing raider
and a body of Union troops, but after traveling at
the rate of thirty-five miles a day, Morgan pulled
up safely within the Confederate lines in northern
Georgia. Fighting on through that winter, he
returned from the mountains into Kentucky the
following spring to recommence his career of
plunder and rapine, but the Union troops forced
him back into Tennessee, where, at Greenville, he
and his staff were surrounded at the house of a
Mrs. Williams, in whose garden—so history says—
the raider was shot dead on September 4, 1864,
while trying to escape.

But Dame Rumor would have it that the wily
raider only feigned death in order to escape his
captors. According to the most persistent story,

members of a secret order assisted him in his escape, and after keeping him in hiding until after the war, maintained secrecy as to his later movements. He is said to have settled in Marion County, Kansas, to have there assumed the name of "Dr. John M. Cole" and to have married. Later he is alleged to have taken his family to Oklahoma, where he died in 1899, being buried near Vian.

Four years ago a reunion of Civil War veterans held at Guthrie, Okla., was addressed by a Mrs. L. F. Larue, who, after confirming these allegations, asserted that she was the daughter of General Morgan by the wife whom he married following his escape into Kansas.

Walton Dwight

Two years after the close of the Civil War there came to Binghamton, N. Y., a yellow-bearded giant who called himself Walton Dwight. He appeared to be very rich and rented the mansion of former United States Senator Daniel B. Dickinson. His new neighbors immediately began to pry into his past history, and, according to what they gathered, he had been born in Winsdor, N. Y., thirty years before. He had entered the Civil War with the Second Pennsylvania Bucktails, had fought bravely for the Union, had risen to the rank of lieutenant-colonel, had been twice wounded at Gettysburg and finally honorably discharged on account of his disabilities. Following his discharge, he had speculated in lumber at Williamsport, Pa., and had become a partner of the famous Peter Herdic. Then he had returned to the place of his birth, at Winsdor, and there married the daughter of a rich farmer.

He was six feet two inches tall and weighed two hundred and fifty pounds. His beard was long and bushy. After some time he purchased a residence of his own and insured it at an unusually heavy figure. One night, when he and his family were in New York, the house mysteriously caught fire and burned to the ground. Some gossips accused him of incendiarism, but the insurance was paid, and with it he began to promote lavish developments in Binghamton. He laid out a park, built forty cottages and a hotel, named after himself, the Dwight House. In a short while he boasted of being a millionaire.

His hobby was insurance, and he took out big life policies, upon which he directly began to negotiate heavy loans. He is said to have borrowed $30,000 from one company, $40,000 from another, $50,000 from a third and various amounts from others. Then came the awful financial panic of 1873. He went down before the avalanche and filed a petition in bankruptcy, rating his liabilities at $400,000. Deserted now by the friends who had enjoyed his opulence, he set off for Chicago and attempted to start life over again, but failure continued to lurk at his door.

Five years after the panic he returned to Winsdor, glowing with health. He now took out life insurance policies aggregating $256,000, and, despite his excellent physical condition, had built for himself an elaborate brick-lined tomb. Then he made a will, leaving many bequests to persons, some of whom, it was later charged, he was to use as tools to carry into effect the most stupendous insurance swindle on record. His extraordinary behavior now began to excite much gossip. He appeared to be either courting death or pretending to subject himself to dangers that might account for future rumors of his demise. In midwinter he would swim icy streams, climb snow-clad peaks and return apparently exhausted from long cross-country walks. One insurance company sent an agent to tender him the amount of the premium which he had paid in and to cancel the policy, but Colonel Dwight, knowing his rights, haughtily declined. At the Fifth Avenue Hotel, New York, about this time, he greatly surprised a friend by claiming a serious illness, despite the fact that he still appeared in good health.

Shortly after this, Dwight moved into a small cottage in Binghamton, went to bed, complained of chills, had a friend stay up with him all night, had his beard and hair trimmed, and the next day was reported to have died in the presence of a former law partner and of a brother-in-law. Mrs. Dwight, who was staying at a hotel next door, was summoned, as were the hotel proprietor and one of his guests. All who saw Dwight lying in his bed attested to his being dead. For two days his body lay in this room, upon which had been placed a Yale lock. The only key was in the hands of the hotel proprietor. A physician stated that Dwight had died of gastritis, but physicians representing the insurance companies maintained that he had killed himself. Some of them claimed to have found the imprint of a rope about his neck.

Belief in Dwight's death, either from suicide or from natural causes, would have been universal had it not been for a little bottle found upon the ground under his window. Upon its label was the word "Gelsemium." Although this mysterious drug was almost unknown to the physicians of Dwight's day, there were some who learned that its effect was to paralyze the motor nerves without the loss of consciousness and to thus produce temporarily an absolute simulation of death.

Medico-legal authorities, considering the possibility of Juliet's suspended animation in the tomb where Romeo found her, have held that "gelsemium" would have produced her deathlike trance.

To account for certain happenings apparently corroborative of Dwight's death, many interesting theories have been advanced. One was that after recovering from the drug, he had been smuggled to some country and a corpse from a New York medical college substituted for his live body; also that the autopsy thought to have been performed upon Dwight was really performed upon this cadaver, one very essential feature of the operation having been the severing of the scalp across the top of the head and pulling it down over the features so as to mask them.

A few months after Dwight's reported death, a man who had shared an office with him was absolutely certain that he met him on the street in Chicago. This appearance immediately gave rise to further theories as to his means of escape, one of them being that he had had himself placed in a box and thus shipped out of Binghamton to a place where confederates had unpacked him and set him at liberty to enjoy a generous share of the insurance money handed back to him by some of those whom he had named as his legal heirs. One of the big companies which had insured his life made immediate payment without contest, but another made a bitter fight, which was pending in the New York courts for many years.

Whether Dwight escaped, hanged himself, died of carefully planned exposure, or from natural causes will in all probability never be known.

Sir Hector Macdonald

Sir Hector Macdonald, "Fighting Mac," was a generation ago the idol of the British soldiers in the Sudan. He was one of Scotland's military heroes who arose from the ranks and the humbler walks of life. The son of a Scotch day laborer, he began life as a barefoot plowboy, later becoming a salesman in a country store. Almost from the cradle he wanted to be a soldier, and when he was a small lad a retired veteran of his native village taught him the rudiments of military tactics. As soon as he was old enough he enlisted as a private in the famous Gordon Highlanders and until he was twenty-six carried the musket of a private soldier. Opportunity knocked first at his door during the Afghan campaign in 1879. Being with a small body of men who found themselves ambushed by two thousand bloodthirsty natives, Macdonald took command of his comrades and led them in a brilliant bayonet charge that drove off the enemy. As this charge not only saved Macdonald's little band, but exposed a plot to annihilate Lord Roberts and his staff, that general offered "Fighting Mac" in return for his bravery a choice of a commissioned officer's straps or the prized Victoria Cross, Macdonald chose the officer's commission. He now piled success upon success. During the Sudan campaign, while only a colonel, he showed distinguished bravery by thwarting a Dervish charge upon the British flank—an action which prevented a serious defeat. His successes were repeated during the Boer War, when, as a reward for a long catalogue of victories and brilliant charges he was both knighted and elevated to the rank of brigadier-general.

These successes, of course, provoked jealousy and envy, added to which was the prejudice always felt by British officers for comrades who "smell of the barracks." It is said that Macdonald forfeited true happiness when he left the ranks and became an officer. Being of a hypersensitive nature, he sensed the criticism rankling in the hearts of his brother officers and was given to spells of brooding, which undermined his health. Having suffered from severe wounds and sunstroke, it was not long before he became a nervous wreck. He was in this state when, after the Boer

14

War, he was placed in command of the British army in Ceylon.

Grave charges were preferred against Sir Hector in 1903 while he still held his Ceylon command, and although none of his friends believed him guilty, his morbid state of mind caused him to lose his nerve and run from his enemies rather than hold them at bay. In other words, he asked for leave to return home and it was granted. The Governor of Ceylon, when bidding him farewell, is said to have advised him to disappear during the voyage, as the disgrace entailed by the charges was such that it could never be lived down.

Arriving home Macdonald appeared at the War Office, protesting his innocence. Lord Roberts, believing him, advised him to return to Ceylon with a stiff upper lip and work on in the knowledge that truth would ultimately prevail. Other of his war chiefs demanded that he return to Ceylon and face a court-martial. Whether such an inquiry was definitely ordered or not is unknown.

In any event, "Fighting Mac" left England presumably to return to the Orient.

Proceeding only as far as Paris, he registered at a hotel, remaining in hiding for a period, during which it was noticed that he was in a highly nervous state. Then one day the British newspapers came out with the shocking intelligence that Sir Hector's corpse had been found in the Paris hotel with a bullet hole through the head. It was said that just previous to the suicide he had been seen reading an English newspaper, which had caused him to burst into tears and hurry to his room. An examination of the newspaper proved that it recounted in great detail the charges preferred against him.

Suspicious events were now about to befall. It was generally supposed that Sir Hector was a bachelor, but when representative members of his family reached Paris to claim his body, they were told that the dead hero's widow had appeared and hurried the corpse to Scotland. There was a public agitation in favor of a military funeral, but it was given out that the widow would not allow the army and navy to do honor to the dead hero. Later it was announced that his funeral had taken place privately at a very early hour in the morning.

Gradually there leaked out the rumor that Sir Hector had taken the advice of the Governor of Ceylon and had disappeared, the suicide story and a mock funeral having been engineered with the assistance of friends. The Mikado having once offered Macdonald a handsome salary and royal honors if he would come to Japan and modernize his army, it was suspected by some that "Fighting Mac," after his alleged escape from disgrace, secretly presented himself at the imperial palace at Tokio and accepted the Mikado's offer. It was rumored at one time that the great Japanese hero, General Kuroki, was, in fact, Sir Hector.

Whether he committed suicide or disappeared, Macdonald ran from the bugaboo that oppressed him and took his desperate step with a clean conscience. Immediately after his alleged death, a commission of inquiry delved into the charges against him and found that they were entirely groundless—that he had been a victim of circumstantial evidence. But no inquiry has ever been able to solve the mystery of "Fighting Mac's" fate.

CHAPTER IX

Mysteries of the Sea

Captain Kidd and His Treasure

LATE in the seventeenth century, when King William commissioned the Earl of Bellomont as Governor of New York and Massachusetts, he admonished that noble to suppress those flagrant piracies that had become the disgrace of the colonies.

Landing in New York the Earl looked about him for a man of red blood and iron nerve, capable of ridding the sea of its bloodthirsty buccaneers. Captain William Kidd, a retired British navigator living upon a comfortable competency in New York, was recommended to the Governor by Robert Livingston and other citizens of prominence.

Kidd was the son of a non-conformist preacher who, after suffering torture by the boot, had died and left his young offspring to carve out a career for himself. The lad had gone to sea when very young and had soon made himself known as a skipper who knew no fear. Before the new Governor of New York selected him to rid the

sea of its freebooters, he had fought against the
French and had done brave service for the cause
of the American colonies, thus winning an award
from the Council of the City of New York.

The Earl of Bellomont found the retired
skipper more than willing to embark upon his
new mission. At that time life in New York was
not the merry whirl that it is in our time.
There were blue laws that restricted individual
liberty and Kidd had been sighing, of late, for
a more exciting environment. To the Earl of
Bellomont he made the boast that with a single
ship of thirty or forty guns he would sweep off
the face of the mighty deep every pirate craft
that dared fly the "Jolly Roger" twixt the Cape
of Good Hope and the Straits of Malacca.

Bellomont believed Kidd and organized a private company which was to take from the buccaneers of the seven seas all of their booty and
divide it among the King, Captain Kidd, his crew
and a list of noble shareholders, including Lord
Shrewsbury, Lord Romney, Lord Orford, the first
lord of the admiralty, and the keeper of the great
seal. A fund of six thousand pounds was subscribed and Captain Kidd was sent forth upon
his mission in the "Adventure," a galley of two
hundred and eighty-seven tons, armed with thirty
guns. He bore with him not only the customary

letters of marque but two commissions under the great seal—one to act against the French and the other to take pirates.

After cutting a bloody swath off Newfoundland and Nova Scotia Kidd darted off for the Orient whence after three years of captures he returned home by way of the West Indies. Here he arrived with an India ship, said to belong to the Great Mogul and to be chock-full of priceless treasure. Then, under the bright sun of his fourth summer out he came sailing peacefully up our coast in a sloop said to be full to the gunwales with specie, gold, silver and jewels recovered from his numerous victims. After entering Delaware Bay upon a mysterious mission he returned to sea only to put into Long Island Sound, anchoring in Oyster Bay. Next he went to Boston to report to Governor Bellomont but that gentleman very rudely placed him in irons and shipped him with several of his men to England where, on May 24, 1701, he was, with nine of his crew, hanged on Execution Dock.

According to the charges preferred at his trial Captain Kidd, while pretending to hunt down pirates, had turned pirate himself. He was charged also with burning houses, massacring peasantry, brutally treating prisoners and particularly with murdering one of his crew. Some

believed that the noble lords who had backed
Kidd's enterprise made him a scapegoat that
their share in the profits might never be known,
and a Parliamentary inquiry looked into the
charge.   But their lordships were vindicated.

After Kidd's execution booty to the value of
only $70,000 could be recovered from his trove
and no one would believe that this was the total
harvest of his three years' enterprise.   Hence,
since his death every strip of beach along his
various coast routes has been upturned in a
search for the vast hoard which he was believed
to have hidden between the time of his arrival
in the West Indies and his arrest in Boston.   A
search for the Great Mogul's ship was instituted
by Governor Bellomont and one theory was that
she had been taken up the Hudson, run ashore and
burned at the base of the Dunderberg, after all
cargo of value had been carried off and buried.
According to other evidence she was burned off
Haiti after her treasure had been removed to the
sloop in which Kidd returned to New York.

There was a story that after this sloop entered
Delaware Bay a chest loaded with treasure was
taken off her, but evidence as to the spot where
this was buried has ever been vague.   A clue
to the burial of part of her cargo on Gardiner's
Island, Long Island Sound, brought better results,

for diggers here found several bales of goods and the treasure that constituted the bulk of the recovered $70,000. Some said that while Kidd's sloop lay off the island three sister craft received mysterious cargoes from her and proceeded north.

What became of the great bulk of Captain Kidd's treasure remains a mystery that has created more widespread popular interest, has been the motif of more extravagant boyhood dreams and has given inspiration to more lurid fiction plots than any other riddle of history. One favorite theory has been that $10,000,000 in gold, silver and jewels was buried by Kidd's crew in a deep pit upon Oak Island, Nova Scotia. Thousands of dollars spent for excavations upon that island resulted a century ago in a discovery that had the world by the ears for a considerable period. The spades of an army of patient diggers were said to have one day struck a forbidding obstruction and there was revealed a mysterious shaft with oaken platforms. Ninety feet down this pit was found a stone slab containing characters which, when translated, are alleged to have read: "Ten feet below are buried 2,000,000 pounds sterling." As late as seven years ago a New York engineer renewed the excavations in this same shaft. But his efforts were as futile as have been all other attempts to solve the riddle.

The Vanished Tichborne Heir

'Tis an unwise mother that knows not her own child.

Fifty years ago Henrietta, Lady Tichborne, widow of Sir James, baronet of that name, fell upon the neck of a prodigal whom she identified as her lost offspring, the heir to the Tichborne title and estates. And thereby her ladyship precipitated a world-wide sensation, also a trial lasting one hundred and eighty-eight days and costing $1,000,000. It was the longest English trial of record.

The strange story begins a century ago with Sir Edward ´Tichborne, baronet, whose estate yielded $100,000 a year. There being no sons to bless him, his heir to the title was a nephew, James, with two sons, Roger and Alfred—two Parisianized youths, whose mother hated England. Roger, the elder boy, prospective heir to the Tichborne baronetcy and estates, was betrothed to his Cousin Katherine, but, being as wild a young subaltern as ever wore a sword at his hip, was required to go abroad for a couple of years' probation before he might claim the hand of his lovely fiancée.

Thus it was, in 1852, that young Roger resigned his commission in the army and sailed for South America to begin life anew in the open. For more than a year he wandered restlessly from place to place, through Latin-America, until hearing that his granduncle had died, that his father had succeeded to the baronetcy and that he was now heir to the title. Thereupon he sailed homeward from Rio Janeiro on the ship "Bella," which mysteriously disappeared at sea. His mother, the aforementioned Lady Henrietta, absolutely refused to believe that he had failed to escape whatever ill fate might have overtaken the "Bella." She had a "presentiment" that he was still alive and that he would one day return to her, but while she continued to reiterate this belief and to persistently advertise for him, offering a handsome reward for knowledge of his whereabouts, her husband died, leaving the baronetcy to her younger son, Alfred, a minor.

Fourteen years after Lady Tichborne had bid her son Roger farewell one of her advertisements brought her a clue. A wanderer located in Australia, and living under the name of Thomas Castro, was said to bear an unmistakable resemblance to her vanished Roger. Through a detective agency he was brought to her in Paris, and here it was she fell upon the neck of her alleged prodigal son, for whom the fatted calf was not only killed, but stuffed, garnished and cooked to a turn. Lady Tichborne faced no danger of having the estates go out of her immediate family, inasmuch as her son Alfred was already the recognized heir to the title. But her identifying the man from Australia aroused a storm of resentment, resulting, as we have said, in the famous Tichborne trial, which she did not live to witness.

At this dramatic hearing many of the lost Roger's friends, relatives and brother officers, also men who had served under him in the ranks, identified the quondam Castro as unmistakably the lost Tichborne heir. To the witness stand, in his behalf, also came sailors from the "Bella" who took oath that they had taken him from the wreck of that vessel. One Jean Luie, a Dane, swore that he had been steward of the American ship "Osprey," which, some five thousand miles off Brazil, in April, 1854, had picked up a ship's boat from the "Bella," containing five sailors and a delirious, helpless man who later called himself "Rogers." The "Osprey" had landed this man at Melbourne, Australia. He and the claimant to the Tichborne baronetcy were positively one and the same. Other witnesses identified a wound on the head of the claimant, also a brown mark upon his side, as having been borne also by the lost Sir Roger.

But after all of this convincing testimony had seemed to filch the title and estates from the young lad, Alfred Tichborne, that youth's counsel played a trump card and thereby caused the hundreds of spectators in the court-room to sit with bated breath. It was a sealed envelope alleged to have been given by Roger to his Cousin Katherine when he sailed for South America and which had never been broken open. The man from Australia when asked to describe its contents swore that before his disappearance he had betrayed his fiancée and that the envelope had contained instructions for her care in case of certain eventualities.

The counsel for the defense then defiantly broke the seal, opened the packet and produced a note which read:

"If God spares me to return and marry my beloved Kate within three years, I promise to build a church and to dedicate it to the Blessed Mother."

This disclosure lost the suit to the alleged Sir Roger. Branded as a vilifier, a defamer and a cad, he was tried for perjury and, being found guilty, spent ten years in prison. After gaining his freedom he came to New York, embarked upon a lecture tour, failed in the enterprise, became a bartender in a Chatham Square saloon, returned penniless to England and there saved himself from starvation by accepting a commission from a newspaper to write his "confession," an extravagant statement whose details few believed, although it admitted his claim to the Tichborne titles to have been fraudulent.

Somewhere between this man's extravagant admissions of guilt and the story that Roger Tichborne had been lost at sea lay the truth. What was it? And why should the lost Roger's mother have tried to foist him upon British aristocracy if by so doing she would have taken $100,000 a year and a baronetcy from her own son?

The Tichborne claimant died on April 1, 1898, leaving a daughter, Theresa, who, about fifteen years later, still entertained such bitterness over her father's loss of his case that she sent a threatening letter to the fiancée of Sir Alfred's grandson, the present baronet.

What was the secret behind Lady Tichborne's recognition of the prodigal from Australia? It seems to have died with that woman of mystery.

The "Marie Celeste"

Of all the skippers that have sailed the seven seas, Captain B. S. Briggs, of the Yankee bark "Marie Celeste," has been the cause of the most speculation. Nautical experts, savants and literary geniuses of world repute have attempted to solve the riddle which he left in his uncertain wake—a wake which has led everywhere and nowhere upon the face of the mighty deep.

With a stanch hull and strong rig the "Marie Celeste," on November 7, 1873, sailed from New York for Genoa with a cargo of alcohol in casks. Captain Briggs hailed from Marion, Mass. He took along his wife and two-year-old baby. The bark's two mates and one man of her crew were Americans. The other four men in her forecastle were Germans. According to her log she passed the island of St. Mary's, in the Azores, on the 24th of November. Ten days later the British bark "Dei Gratia," bound from New York to Gibraltar, sighted her drifting aimlessly about under partial sail. Suspicious of her eccentric behavior, Captain Boyce, of the "Dei Gratia," hailed her, but received no response. Boarding her, he made a discovery that set his jaws agape and his eyes staring. It was not a scene of blood and carnage, but a spectacle so peaceful that it was uncanny. The "Marie Celeste" had been mysteriously abandoned in the open sea.

Bad weather had not caused her crew to leave her. A bottle of medicine was standing upright on the skipper's table, where a moderately heavy sea would have upset it. Pirates had not frightened Captain Briggs and his comrades away. The cargo was undisturbed and in the forecastle were the sailors' chests, filled with their clothing and money, untouched. Skipper Briggs' gold watch hung beside his berth.

Starvation had not threatened. There was plenty of food. In the galley victuals had been prepared for the next meal. There was also plenty of water. And all about was searoom enough for a considerable cruise. No shoals or rocky coasts were near.

Yet there was every indication of a sudden, although peaceful, abandonment of the ship. Upon the log slate, following the usual routine entries, had been scrawled:

"Fanny, my dear wife——"

The entry was unfinished. Apparently, the event causing the ship's abandonment had come while the skipper was writing it. Was it to have been an account of something untoward that had befallen his spouse? And was this emergency the cause of every one's suddenly leaving the vessel? Mrs. Briggs had hurriedly dropped her sewing. Upon her table in the cabin were threaded needle, scissors and a bit of partly sewed material, lying as if hastily tossed aside. On the open melodeon lay music that had apparently been played since the cabin was last put to rights. There was still the impression left by a baby's head upon the pillow in the crib and toys were strewn about on the cabin floor.   On the wall the clock still ticked.

The fore hatch was open, but whether one of the boats had been launched was a matter of doubt.   If none was put to sea all aboard the "Marie Celeste" must either have gone into the sea or had been taken aboard some other craft. Yet in all of the intervening years no boat has reported visiting her.   And why should it?   She was in excellent condition, ready to proceed on her cruise.   If Captain Briggs, his family and crew did embark in one of his ship's boats it would probably have been sighted at sea or upon some beach even after it had overturned and drowned its human frieght.

No signs of storm.   No evidence of famine. No shortage of water.   No fear of a dangerous coast.   No evidence of piratical attack.   No relics of mutiny, struggle or bloodshed.   No leakage and nothing wrong with stearing gear, rigging or navigating paraphernalia.   What is the answer?

The owner, the late J. H. Winchester, of Rahway, N. J., could never venture a solution. Neither could Messrs. Meisner, Ackermann & Co., the New York firm to whom she was chartered.   Many fanciful theories as to the fate of her vanished occupants have been offered.   Ac-

15

cording to one, Captain Briggs became insane as the result of rough weather encountered in the open sea. But, granting that he did, were there not seven able-bodied men aboard, capable of resisting his crazy commands? According to another theory, the casks rattling about in the hold sprang a leak and the resulting alcohol fumes, threatening to smother those on board, caused their hasty exodus. But the evidence says that the cargo was intact.

Some would attribute the bark's abandonment to the log slate's vague evidence that some misadventure, some untoward happening, threatened the life of Mrs. Briggs. But if illness or any other danger threatened her, why would her husband, an experienced navigator, take her to sea in an open boat when he had a perfectly good and absolutely seaworthy vessel at his command?

The "Marie Celeste" was taken in hand by Captain Boyce and the crew of the "Dei Gratia." They sailed her to Gibraltar as a prize and she eventually fell into the hands of a skipper who, a dozen years later, was alleged to have run her upon a reef in order to collect insurance for her owners.

Superstitious mariners believe that she had been cursed. Some doubted whether her baptism had been performed with real wine.

The secret of her abandonment by Skipper

CAPTAIN BRIGGS BECAME INSANE

Briggs remains one of the blackest of the world's nautical mysteries.

Johann Salvator—The Lost Grand Duke

In the late eighties there dwelt in the suburbs of Vienna a shopkeeper, Emil Stubel, whose three pretty daughters went upon the stage.   One golden summer day the Stubel family were attending a picnic in the woods and were partaking of a jolly repast when their gaieties were interrupted by the arrival of a tall and handsome, stately and dashing, but ravenously hungry hunter, on horseback.   The intruder was invited to share the picnic luncheon and as a result of the chance acquaintance he fell in love, at first sight, with the shopkeeper's youngest daughter, Ludmilla.

An ardent courtship ensued.   Fraulein Ludmilla's lover introduced himself as John Orth, a poor student of Gmunden and she addressed his letters thus.   Inasmuch as he received them, as proved by his prompt replies, she did not suspect his truthfulness.   She was very happy until one day her cousin, Max Mahler, a resident of Gmunden, came on a visit to her father and gave the family a shock by stating that no one by the name of Orth lived in his home town, although one of the landmarks of that village was the Castle

of Orth.   And as a result of her cousin Max's
disclosures, corroborated by subsequent investigation, the beautiful Ludmilla sank into a profound melancholy.   Some time afterward while
attending a grand review of the imperial troops
she happened to see a familiar figure riding with
the Emperor's suite and garbed in the resplendent
uniform of a lieutenant field marshal.   It was
none other than her huntsman-lover.

"Who is that big fellow?" asked Herr Stubel
of someone in the crowd.

"Why that is the Archduke Johann Salvator,
son of the late Leopold II, ruler of Tuscany,
nephew of the Queen of Spain and the Empress of
Brazil, also cousin of our Emperor," replied the
bystander.

The lovely Ludmilla sank into deeper melancholy.   She sent her lover word that she would
see him no more.

Archduke Johann Salvator was born in the
famous Pitti Palace, in Florence, but when a lad
of seven was driven hence with his family by
the Franco-Italian armies which overturned his
father's throne.   His cousin, the Emperor Franz-
Josef, of Austria-Hungary, took the ex-ruler of
Tuscany under his protection and Johann Salvator grew to be a dashing figure at the court of
Vienna.   He was endowed with unusual intelli-

gence—a profound knowledge of chemistry, a
genius for poetry and a talent for music. Various
volumes of his writings were published under his
pen name, John Orth, and he composed waltzes,
ballets and even operas that were produced and
pronounced immensely successful. Time never
lagged when he was about. The court balls
held in the gorgeous Rittersaal of the Hofburg
were not a success unless his Apollo-like form was
seen towering above the multitude.

All went well with Johann until he presumed
to take a hand in politics. His writings became
too radical for the conservatives that hedged
about his imperial cousin, and when he urged
an alliance between Austria and Russia to coun-
teract the growing hostility of Germany, Kaiser
Wilhelm protested so urgently that Franz-Josef
had to discipline his obstreperous young cousin.
So Johann was placed under arrest and transferred from the artillery to the infantry. It was
about this time that Ludmilla Stubel had cried
her eyes out at the discovery that he was not her
dreamed of beggar student but a prince of the
imperial blood.

As a result of his tribulations, Johann Salvator
became disgusted with court life. He resigned
his lofty rank in the army, stripped himself of
the titles "Archduke of Austria," "Prince of

Hungary," "Grand Ducal Prince of Tuscany" and "Knight of the Golden Fleece." Converting a large part of his estate into cash he shocked the imperial court by running off and marrying the lovely Ludmilla Stubel. At London he chartered a bark, the "Margherita," engaged a captain and crew and taking his bride along sailed in this craft as second mate, that he might be nearer in spirit to the men aboard, who knew him only by his pen name, John Orth. Little did they guess that he was an imperial prince.

The "Margherita" cruised between Buenos Aires and Valparaiso for awhile, engaged in the nitrate of soda trade. On July 13, 1890, she left Buenos Aires ostensibly to sail around the Horn and back to Valparaiso, but was never definitely heard of again although since that time the Grand Duke Johann Salvator has been reported in a score or more of places.

He has become one of the most unfathomable mysteries of modern times.

Where is he? And what has become of his beautiful Ludmilla?

According to affidavits collected from eye-witnesses by Eugenio Garzon, a former senator of Uruguay, Johann Salvator, for some mysterious reason, halted his vessel at a lonely place, painted out her name, sailed her up the Uruguay

River, sold her, paid off her crew and disappeared. In 1897 he was reported as fighting with the Congressionalists in the Chilean War. About ten years ago Dr. Manuel Quintana, son of a former president of Argentina, reported that he had just sailed from Buenos Aires to Cherbourg with Archduke Johann, on the steamer "Araguaya." About a year later a former private under the lost Grand Duke's command reported having seen him and his wife at the Hotel Arcadia, San Monica, Cal. Others have "identified" Johann as Admiral Yamagata, of the Japanese navy, as a ranchman in Argentina and as the leader of a new thought sect in Tacoma, Washington.

Whatever the fate of Johann Salvator, his cousin, the Emperor of Austria, always believed him to be still alive, for only shortly before that monarch died he issued an edict that the $8,000,000 estate of his vagabond cousin be held intact until 1917.

CHAPTER X

Where Murder Would Not Out

Hippolyte Menaldo

BUT what I want you to tell me, Maria, is the name of my mother. You don't know how worried I feel. The other boys all have mothers. Their mothers write to them, they write to their mothers. I feel as if I can't go on working. I wish you would come and see me."

To his beloved nurse, Maria Chaix, thus wrote one of the most tragic figures of modern times, Hippolyte Menaldo, after being torn from her to go away to school.

Maria Chaix, a poor dressmaker of Orleans, had been a foster mother to this child ever since, when only a few days old, he had been brought to her by certain mysterious and wealthy persons to whom she had been recommended by the parish priest. Thereafter the tender and faithful Maria received a monthly income for the infant's support, also regular visits from a grande dame of the old aristocracy, often accompanied by a beautiful girl, who, although still in her teens,

(233)

displayed a maternal interest in the baby.   But
Maria Chaix was never to know the identity of her
foster-child or of her visitors.   All that she knew
of little Hippolyte was her love for him that
multiplied with every pound that he gained.
And it broke her heart when, at the age of twelve,
he was visited by his guardian, Monsieur Martin,
who took him suddenly from her and placed him in
a school, at Savoy, where he was to be educated
for the priesthood and whose headmaster was
strictly forbidden to give him any information
concerning his real name or origin.

At school Hippolyte became so melancholy that
he had to be sent away, now and then, for vaca-
tions in the country.   As indicated by his letters
to his beloved nurse, he brooded over the uncertainty of his identity, and this state of mind so far
took possession of him that one day when sent
upon a long cross-country walk with his schoolmates, he ran away to earn money with which
he proposed to find his mother.   After wandering
through the country for two weeks, he was
discovered on the road to Orleans, and when
returned to school remarked:

"I am determined to know who I am!   I have
a right to know!"

Hippolyte was then fourteen.   After being
returned to school he refused to become a priest

and his guardian, Monsieur Martin, being advised to rearrange his future, told the headmaster that he would send the lad to America.

At his guardian's command Hippolyte Menaldo departed from school, leaving behind his baggage, which was to be sent for when required. It was never sent for. Eight days after his departure fishermen found upon the rocks below Castellamare, near Naples, the body of a youth described by the police as between fourteen and seventeen, as wearing the peculiar uniform of French parochial schools and as having about his neck a medal worn by Roman Catholic pupils. Identifying marks had been cut or picked out of all of his clothing, except his stockings, which bore the number fifty-six.

Cab drivers plying the sea road near where the corpse was found remembered that two nights before its discovery they had seen upon that highway a distinguished-looking man leading a lad who was in such a pitiful state of exhaustion that they had offered the pair a lift. Their services were declined by the man who an hour later was seen on the same road alone. After the police had searched in vain for the mysterious stranger the body was buried and the incident forgotten.

Nine years later the wealthy Marquise de

Nayve, dwelling in the suburbs of Paris, astonished
the local Procureur by calling upon him one
Sunday and stating that, to ease her conscience,
she must confess her suspicion that her husband,
the Marquis, had once murdered an illegitimate
son whom she had had by a former suitor before her
marriage, when she was but a child of sixteen.
Investigation instituted by the astonished Procureur identified this child as the unhappy
Hippolyte Menaldo, and the Marquise and her
mother as the two ladies of rank who had visited
the child during the happy days that he had
spent with his nurse in Orleans.

Arrested and tried for the murder of Hippolyte
Menaldo, the Marquis de Nayve put up a remarkable defense. According to this story, his wife's
parents had confessed her youthful folly to him
when they had become betrothed and he had
not only forgiven her readily, but after their
marriage had agreed to masquerade as the unhappy child's guardian, Monsieur Martin, the
better to look after his interests.

At the trial there was produced a letter which
the Marquis had written to the Marquise from
Marseilles immediately after the disappearance
of Hippolyte. In this he had fully explained that
while attempting to give Hippolyte a pleasant
holiday upon the eve of his departure for America,

he had taken the lad to Rome and Florence and finally to Naples, where they were walking out on the sea road when, after violently objecting to the American trip, the boy had suddenly run off in the darkness and had mysteriously disappeared. In the same letter the Marquis had inclosed a press clipping describing the finding of the mysterious corpse near the sea road.

The evidence further proved that the Marquis de Nayve, after returning home, had not acted as a guilty man, but, instead, had called in the parish priest and two lawyers, explaining to them what had happened and asking their advice, which was that, under the circumstances, he absolutely remain silent. He had also received the same advice from the headmaster of the Savoy Seminary, where Hippolyte had studied. So the truth had lain buried until the Marquise's morbid broodings had led to the suspicions which she felt duty bound to make public.

After the distracted Marquise had, in the witness box, admitted that she had no proofs to back up her suspicions, and after several of Hippolyte's schoolmates had sworn that they had heard him threaten suicide, the jury brought in a verdict of "Not guilty!"

A week later the Marquise returned to her husband, and thereafter they lived happily with their charming daughter and two handsome sons. But Paris has never ceased to wonder as to the truth behind the strange case.

The Strange Case of Marie Lafarge

The most baffling of all French murder mysteries involved the daughter of one of Napoleon's favorite officers, Colonel Cappelle, of the Old Guard. This beautiful girl was also the granddaughter of the famous Duke of Orleans (Philippe Egalite) and of his companion and housekeeper, Mme. de Genlis.

Marie Cappelle had a very lonely girlhood. After her father's death, when she was very young, her mother remarried, and she was adopted by her aunt. Many men sought her hand, but she failed to return their love, and continued to endure her secluded existence until the age of twenty-three, when, influenced by her uncle, she consented to a marriage of convenience with Charles Lafarge, a young ironmaster, who lived with his mother in a lonely country house, Les Glandiers.

On the day of their return from their honeymoon Marie locked herself in her room and slipped under the door to her entreating husband a note asking him to free her from her vows, as she loved another and could not endure the contemplation

of a life at Les Glandiers. But the couple became
reconciled and circumstances seemed to indicate
that the story of the former lover was a fiction
invented by Marie. Thereafter she took her place
in Lafarge's home, furthered his interests and
made herself beloved by his employees and
neighbors.

Lafarge was a man of hot temper, and it soon
developed that he was not altogether honest in his
business transactions. But Marie continued to
transform the ugly country house into a cheerful
home and to bring sunshine even into the soul of
her grim mother-in-law, who had disliked her
from the first. After some time the young bride
fell ill. Calling her husband to her bedside, she
told him that as evidence of her love and devotion
she wished to make a will leaving him the sole
enjoyment of her fortune, and Lafarge, touched
by her act, made a will of his own, leaving her
everything that he possessed. Finally, to raise
money for the development of a new enterprise,
the ironmaster went to Paris, taking with him one
Denis, a foreman. This sinister individual seemed
to exert an evil influence over Lafarge and to share
some knowledge that gave him power over his
employer. Lafarge remained away more than a
month, during which time he and his wife ex-
changed affectionate letters. In one of these

missives she told her husband that she had sent
to him a box containing a miniature of herself
and a few little cakes which she had made, requesting that he eat one at midnight, at which hour she,
according to an ancient custom, would eat a
similar one herself as a pledge of their love.

The box arrived at Lafarge's hotel and was
opened not by himself, but by a servant. Afterward, according to his own testimony, the box,
when presented to him, contained not the several
small cakes described by his wife, but one large
one. Eating a piece of it, he was taken violently
ill. With Denis, he then returned home, having
negotiated a loan of $2,000, which transaction was
carefully concealed from Marie. His illness con-
tinuing, Marie was in constant attendance at his
bedside. As his sleep was continually interrupted
by rats infesting the old home, she, as on previous
occasions, ordered arsenic for their extermination,
and Denis procured it from the chemist.

Lafarge suffered a painful illness, supposed to
be due to attacks of colic, to which he had been
subjected since childhood. Finally there arrived
upon the scene one Mme. Brun, an intimate of
Marie's mother-in-law. The ironmaster now grew
worse and Marie begged that a famous specialist
be called in for consultation, but his mother
insisted upon engaging a young, inexperienced

physician.   Lafarge died, and after Marie had
retired to her room to give way to her grief she
was amazed to find herself locked in.   It then
developed that as a result of insinuations made by
Mme. Brun she had been suspected of poisoning
her husband.   Mme. Brun and Mme. Lafarge, the
elder, claimed to have suspected Marie's guilt for
some days before her husband's death, yet they
had meanwhile continued to allow her to prepare
his food.   Medical experts, who made a post-
mortem upon Lafarge, reported that they had
found no trace of poison in his body, whereupon
his mother apologized for having suspected Marie,
but the authorities did not seem to be satisfied, and the widow, now only twenty-four years
old, was subjected to a rigid examination, during
which her enemies, Mme. Brun and Denis, pointed
the finger of suspicion against her.   As a result
Marie, a bride of less than one year, was taken
to prison.

While awaiting trial the unhappy woman was
subjected to another shock.   The public prosecutor received a letter signed "Marquis de
Liautaud" and begging that the Lafarge chateau
be searched for valuable diamonds belonging to his
wife.   Now it happened that the young Marquise
de Liautaud had been Marie's girlhood chum and
confidante and that she had visited the Lafarges

16

soon after their marriage. French society was shocked when the diamonds described were found in Marie's dressing case. Considering the wealth of the families concerned, this incident became a mystery that deepened with the fair suspect's repeated statements to her attorney that she could not explain the apparent theft even to him.

The young widow was, however, tried for the theft while still awaiting trial for the murder. At length she confessed to her attorney that the Marquise had selected her as a go-between to sell her diamonds and with the money meet the demands of a former lover, who had threatened to blackmail her. But this story was not believed by the jurors and Mme. Lafarge was convicted of stealing her friend's gems. All France now divided into two camps—the Lafargists and anti-Lafargists. But the diamond case proved to be the young widow's undoing. Her subsequent murder trial lasted seventeen days and resulted in her conviction. She was sentenced to the pillory and the guillotine. Protests poured into the government from all over the country, and finally, on account of public opinion, her sentence was commuted to life imprisonment.

While she languished in prison it developed that just at the time when, according to her testimony, the Marquise de Liautaud was being blackmailed, a French official bearing the same name as the blackmailer had received from Paris a mysterious box expressed by some one named Liautaud, to whom it was returned unopened. With this new testimony, the prisoner's counsel attempted to reopen the case, but she had languished in prison for twelve years before being finally pardoned. She then retired to a secluded watering place, where, five months after regaining her freedom, she died.

Two famous German authorities on criminal jurisprudence wrote an exhaustive treatise setting forth the conclusion that the real murderer of Lafarge had been the evil Denis. The blackmailer in the case died in a madhouse about the time of Marie's death.

Guilelma Sands

One of the most famous and perplexing of America's murder mysteries came to light in the environs of New York city during Christmas week, 1799.

Ellis Ring, a Quaker, and his wife, Catharine, dwelt in a farmhouse occupying the present site of the Franklin Street station of the Ninth Avenue elevated railroad. Living with them as boarders were Mrs. Ring's sister, Hope Sands; her cousin, Guilelma Sands and Levi Weeks, a master car-

penter. The Sands girls had come to the Ring
farm early in the autumn, and within three weeks
after their arrival, Guilelma, a maiden of ravishing
beauty, had embarked upon a love affair with
Weeks.   As her suitor was a young man of
excellent prospects, brother of the owner of the
City Hotel, on Broadway, the Rings did not dis-
courage his attentions to their pretty cousin.

On the night of December 29th, Guilelma
announced to Mrs. Ring that she and Weeks
contemplated being married privately that night.
Weeks, who had gone out of the house after supper
that evening, returned at about eight o'clock, at
which time Mrs. Ring, on going upstairs, found
Guilelma dressed, ready to go out.   Returning
to the lower floor, Mrs. Ring then found Weeks
standing in the entry, but, without disturbing
him, she went into the sitting-room.   A moment
later she heard some one descend the stairs, after
which the front door was opened and closed.
Thereupon Mrs. Ring ran to the door and looked
out.   As there were many people passing she could
not distinguish Guilelma or Weeks among them.

At ten o'clock that evening Weeks returned to
his boarding house.   Mrs. Ring was still up and
he asked her if Guilelma had gone to bed.   Mrs.
Ring replied that her young cousin had gone out
and had not returned, whereupon Weeks expressed

his surprise that she had stayed out so late. Mrs.
Ring said that Guilelma had not gone out alone,
and in reply to Weeks' inquiry as to whom she
had gone with, the Quaker housewife exclaimed:

"Indeed, Levi, to tell thee the truth, I believe
she went out with thee."

"If she had gone out with me," answered
Weeks, "she would have come in with me."

Mrs. Ring sat up almost throughout the
remainder of the night, but Guilelma Sands did
not return. Weeks, who shared her vigil, seemed,
as she described it, unnatural and moody. Indeed,
at one time he broke down and cried out that if
Guilelma did not reappear to clear him he was a
ruined man.

According to the testimony of some one who
claimed to have seen her, Guilelma entered a
sleigh when she left the Ring house, and that was
all that was known as to her departure from her
home. Chancellor Ferris, of the New York
University, writing to a historian in 1861, said:

"An old aunt of mine, who knew her (Guilelma
Sands) well and who saw her on the night of the
fatal sleigh ride when she was just ready to step
into the sleigh, always spoke of her as the most
lovely creature she ever saw, and especially
fascinating at that moment."

A few days after Guilelma's disappearance her

muff was found in the lonely Lispenard meadow
in a well which the Manhattan Company had
dug to supply a part of New York city with water.
On January 2d a search of the bottom of the well-
revealed Miss Sands' body.   Her hat was off,
her shoes and stockings had been pulled from her
feet and her clothing above the waist was torn.
There were bruises and discolorations about her
neck.

New York was thrown into an uproar by the
discovery of the body.   A coroner's jury on
January 6th found that the young woman had
come to her death at the hands of a person or
persons unknown, but the public clamored for
vengeance, and, as Weeks was the only one whose
name could possibly be linked with that of the
beautiful victim, he was arrested and brought to
trial.   A post-mortem upon the body showed that
there were no physical reasons why Miss Sands
should have desired to end her life or why Weeks
should have wished to rid himself of her.   Moreover, the young man bore an excellent reputation
for propriety and sobriety of conduct, and Miss
Sands had, immediately before her disappearance,
been in an unusually cheerful mood that offset
any suspicion of a quarrel between her and her
lover.

These points were brought out at Weeks'

trial, which began on March 31, 1800, in the old
City Hall. It was one of the most famous criminal
trials in American history, and the chief actors
were national figures destined to contribute
dramatic incidents to the history of their country.
The trial judge was Chief Justice Lansing, who
was later to figure in one of the most sensational
disappearance mysteries that ever stirred the
metropolis; and the defendant's counsel were
Aaron Burr and Alexander Hamilton, who were
soon afterward to fight their celebrated duel.
So great was the excitement during the trial
that a volunteer guard of prominent citizens
had to be formed to protect the accused while
he was being conveyed between the court-
house and the prison, and it is chronicled that the
street outside the court was so crowded and the
trial rooms so noisy that at times the court
officers had to clear the neighborhood before the
hearing could go on.

There were witnesses who swore that Weeks
had been at his brother's house between 8.30 and
ten o'clock on the night of the tragedy and that he
had shown no undue excitement during the visit.
According to one account, Aaron Burr saved
Weeks by resorting to a sensational trick. Turning aside from his examination of a witness,
he rushed up to an unknown spectator and, with

a pair of lighted candles in his hand, held them
up to the latter's face shouting:

"Gentlemen, here is the real murderer!"

The effect of this dramatic incident was the
mysterious suspect's flight "in virtual acknowl-
edgment of his guilt." When the prosecution
closed its case, it was half-past two in the morning,
and the judge, after refusing to permit adjourn-
ment until the trial was ended, charged the jury
that from the evidence proffered Levi Weeks
could not have murdered Guilelma Sands in the
few minutes that he was away from his brother's
house. The court then recommended a verdict
of "not guilty" and the jury, after four minutes'
deliberation, acquitted the defendant.

The murder was a favorite theme of historians
and other scribes for many years after its occurrence. It afforded the plot of Theodore Fay's
novel, "Norman Leslie." Its solution remains
today as hopeless as it was more than a century
ago.

Madeline Smith

James Smith, a prosperous architect of Glasgow,
Scotland, lived happily with his wife and five
children. The pride of the family was their
elder daughter, Madeline, a belle of twenty,
renowned in society for her exceptional beauty,

charm and cleverness. She was a young woman
of great vitality and vivacity, to whose wondrous
blue eyes many Scotch swains had capitulated.

In March, 1857, Madeline Smith's parents
announced her engagement to William Minnoch,
a man of great integrity and prosperity. On
the day after the announcement of the engagement
the Smiths received a call from a Miss Perry, who
announced the death of Emile Angelier, a young
Frenchman, a former suitor whom Madeline
Smith had dismissed. After the departure of
Miss Perry, who had acted as a go-between in the
love affair with Angelier, the Smiths held evening
prayers and Madeline went to bed with her little
sister in a basement room with barred windows,
which chamber she had occupied since the family
had moved into their present house.

Next morning, when her little sister awoke,
Madeline was missing. She had gotten up before
sunrise, packed a small satchel and taken the
early boat for her father's country house. But
before the sun was barely up Glasgow was agog
with the surprising news that this fair daughter
of one of the city's most eminent residents had
been arrested for the murder of Angelier.

The demeanor of Miss Smith, after her arrest,
made a good impression upon those who followed
her case. She had the bearing of proud innocence

and candor. For two months she remained in prison awaiting her trial and during that interval the whole English-speaking world divided itself into two factions—those believing her a martyr and those branding her as a demon. To insure an impartial trial her case was transferred from Glasgow to Edinburgh, where the most famous legal lights of Great Britain contended for her acquittal and conviction.

According to the testimony presented, Angelier, a poor correspondence clerk in a Glasgow business house, had fallen in love with Madeline Smith at first sight on the street and had arranged an introduction to her through the French Consul General. Realizing that a marriage with the wealthy girl would deliver him from his humble condition, he had arranged frequent interviews through the instrumentality of Miss Perry. Thus Madeline, a girl in her teens, had been led into secret meetings with her first suitor and had been induced to answer a long list of passionate love letters which he stealthily slipped through her barred window. Madeline, responding to the Frenchman's temperament, let her imagination run away with her and indulged herself in a romance at first largely on paper. While she destroyed all of her secret lover's letters, he was careful to keep all of hers, which were framed in the graceful verbiage of a young woman of culture.

After a time the romance commenced to cool and Madeline grew to admire Minnoch, a man of much more substantial character than was her temperamental lover. Angelier thereupon began to utter those jealous complaints that always defeat a lover's purpose, yet Madeline, as a solace, continued to address him in endearing terms. Learning of her engagement to his rival, the Frenchman showed the cad that was in him by threatening to reveal her letters, whereupon the girl became panic-stricken and badly distraught, as her father was one of those stern Scotchmen who would not have hesitated to turn from his door a child who had strayed even slightly from the path of conventionality.

Miss Smith, while addressing to her erstwhile lover frantic appeals to have her letters returned, had sent to a chemist for prussic acid needed ostensibly as a cosmetic and had three times purchased arsenic for the avowed purpose of destroying rats. But her purchases had been made openly and she had signed with her own name the poison book of the apothecary.

The chief witness against the fair prisoner was Miss Perry. She testified to an alleged ante-mortem statement by Angelier that his illness had followed his taking a cup of coffee or cocoa given him by Madeline.

On the night when the poisoning is alleged to have taken place, Angelier's movements could not be accounted for during a period of five hours, while it was proved that Madeline Smith was at home and during the time a policeman watching the neighborhood was positive that no one had approached the window of her room. Physicians who had made the post-mortem upon the young Frenchman testified that he had died from arsenical poisoning. But the attorneys for the beautiful defendant, who from the beginning had shown no sign of guilt or remorse, pointed out that no possible advantage could have been gained by their client through Angelier's death so long as her incriminating letters remained in existence and in his possession; and they laid stress upon the point that any one of her intelligence would have anticipated that Angelier's murder would make her love letters public to the world—as was the case. Her flight upon hearing of his death was pointed to as evidence of her realization that her correspondence would now be found in the foreigner's room. Thus she had left for her father's country house until this publicity might abate. That Angelier had threatened suicide was also brought out in the evidence.

The climax of Madeline Smith's sensational trial was the Scotch verdict—"Not proven."

The case caused an estrangement between her and Minnoch, and later she became the wife of a wealthy and influential Englishman, with whom she shared a long and happy life, whose placidity could hardly have been enjoyed by one tortured by a murderer's guilty conscience.

The Burdell Murder

Harvey Burdell was born on a farm near Herkimer, N. Y., in 1811. Turned adrift by his parents when just entering his teens, he became a typesetter on a country weekly. Then he wandered to New York city, where he studied dentistry in the office of his brother John at Broadway and Chambers Street, upon the present site of the Stewart Building. To complete his dental education he also took a course in medicine.

He was a large, handsome man of powerful frame, with expressive eyes and a full, dark beard. Quarreling with his brother, he set up practice for himself, acquired many patients and grew very rich. After a few years he became engaged to a rich young woman, who, in 1835, dismissed him because in a fit of anger he had struck her father. Thereupon the dentist became engaged to the adopted daughter of a wealthy

18

New Yorker, but after appearing for the wedding
in the presence of the clergyman and guests he
flew into a passion because the father of his bride-
elect would not make a settlement of $20,000 upon
him, and the result of the dispute was the bride's
marrying the best man.

Another woman who figured in Burdell's life
was the widow of George C. Cunningham, who
had died leaving her an insurance of $10,000.
After she had spent this in extravagant living, she
became Burdell's housekeeper.   She brought
to his house two sons and two daughters, all under
age.   She held the premises under nominal
lease and Burdell ostensibly subletted from her
the front parlor on the street floor, also the front
and rear bedrooms on the second story.   The
second-story-front chamber he used as an operating
room and he slept in the rear bedroom.   He kept
one servant, a lad, who served as office boy and
valet and who slept outside the house.   Mrs.
Cunningham kept two other lodgers—John J.
Eckel, a manufacturer, and George V. Snodgrass,
the son of a clergyman.   Doctor Burdell took his
meals at a nearby hotel.

Friday, January 30, 1857, was dark and rainy.
During the afternoon Doctor Burdell received
several patients until five o'clock, when he put on
his long coat and hat, threw a heavy shawl about

his shoulders and stepped out upon the front steps. Raising his umbrella, he looked up and down Bond Street, descended to the pavement and started leisurely toward Broadway.

That was the last seen of him. About eight the next morning, the office boy, entering the operating room with a scuttle of coal, had difficulty in opening the door. Pushing against some object that obstructed it, he looked behind it and was terrified to find the body of Doctor Burdell, with head against it, upon the floor. The corpse was covered with blood that had gushed from many wounds. The dead dentist was fully dressed. There was blood everywhere—on the floor, on the walls, on the furniture, as well as in the hall and upon the upper stairways. The furniture was upset and there were evidences of a desperate struggle. The gas was still burning at full head.

Burdell's features were so distorted that at first his face was almost unrecognizable. About the throat a great welt bore evidence that the dentist had been strangled, and distributed over his body were fifteen stab wounds, narrow and deep, as if made by a long, slender dagger. The doctor's shawl lay upon the lounge and the position of the blood stains upon the floor indicated that he had been seated in a chair by his instrument case when attacked, also that he had been assaulted very soon after entering the room. One murderer had apparently thrown about his neck the cord that had strangled him, while the other had delivered the dagger thrusts.

After trembling in terror at the bloody sight before him, the office boy ran to the dining-room, where he found Mrs. Cunningham, her family and Snodgrass at breakfast. The housekeeper burst into tears when told of the murder and ran to the death chamber, followed by Snodgrass. Eckel had breakfasted early and gone to his factory.

Cries of murder uttered by the cook caused the house to swarm with people. The coroner's investigation indicated that the stab wounds had been made by a left-handed person and, as Mrs. Cunningham was left-handed, she was placed under arrest, as were Snodgrass and Eckel. In the attic of the house of tragedy were found a blood-stained sheet, a man's nightshirt and towel. There were blood stains in the bedroom of Snodgrass, and even upon the pages of a book of poems found upon the piano in the parlor. In the fireplace of the murder chamber were evidences that paper and leather had been burned therein, the fire having been suddenly extinguished by water. The dentist's gold watch and pocketbook were found upon his body and none of his property was missing.

Mrs. Cunningham was placed on trial the first week in May. After the case had lasted only three days she was acquitted and her alleged accomplices were never brought to trial. The strangest chapter in the mystery was now to follow. Mrs. Cunningham put in a claim for the murdered dentist's estate, claiming that she was his widow and, when his heirs contested the claim, more than one hundred and fifty witnesses were called to substantiate her testimony. According to her evidence she had been married to Burdell on October 28, 1856, by Doctor Marvine, of the Dutch Reformed Church, in Bleecker Street. But, according to the Burdell claimants, she had carried out the marriage with a man made up to personate Burdell. Mrs. Cunningham brought forward a child, whom she claimed to have been hers by the murdered man, but, when confronted with evidence that it was not hers, she confessed, and the prosecution was dropped. However, the murder mystery was never cleared up. It remains to this day a subject of debate among criminal lawyers.

Tragedy followed in the wake of the murdered man. His brother died in an insane asylum and Eckel died in the Albany Penitentiary, where he had been imprisoned for whisky frauds. Mrs. Cunningham, after surviving the tragedy thirty years, succumbed to a malady of the brain while

living in poverty and under an assumed name
in an obscure Harlem flat.

Jack the Ripper

There was a reign of terror in London's Whitechapel district during the late eighties. On
Christmas, 1887, a woman of the demi-monde
was brutally murdered and mutilated, and during
1888 seven more crimes of the same character
added to the frenzy of underworld denizens.
Again, in 1889, two more victims were found, and
early in 1891 a twelfth.

All of the victims were of the class known as
street-walkers and all bore the same unmistakable
marks of brutality. The throat of each was cut
and each body upon which the murderer apparently had had time to complete his butchery was
eviscerated in the same manner. It was the
methodical work of some fiend, maniac or monster
who seemed to possess a knowledge of surgery and
anatomy. He always managed to escape, and
apparently there was no motive except a revolting
appetite for butchery or thirst for revenge.
Seemingly he had no ill-will against, or personal
knowledge of, his victims, each of whom was of a
class that he knew would place herself voluntarily
at his mercy and would unconsciously assist him
in avoiding danger of detection.

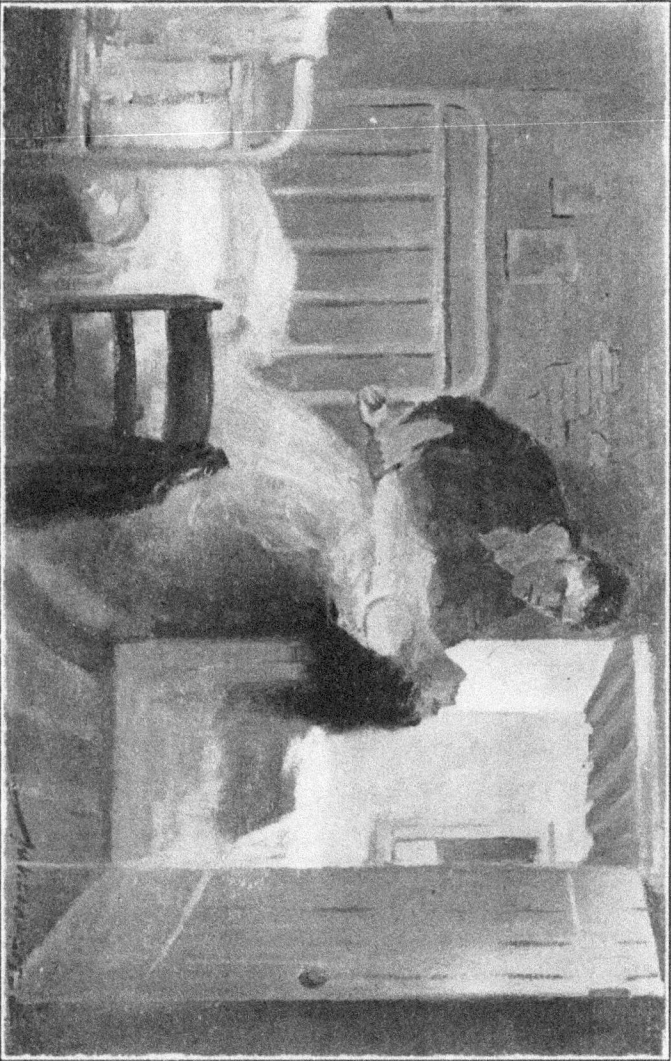

ALL THE VICTIMS BORE THE SAME UNMISTAKABLE MARKS

On the 30th of September, 1888, the monster
murdered two of his victims, one immediately
after the other. The fact that the first whom
he killed was not mutilated in the usual way
indicated that he had been interrupted before
completing his bloody work. And being thus
disturbed before satisfying his mania for mutilation in the accustomed way, he ran out and completed his work upon the next victim whom he
could find.

The police were nonplused from the start.
The fiend appeared to change his lodgings after
each murder. Some newspaper scribe dubbed the
monster "Jack the Ripper" and the name was
soon upon every tongue throughout both Europe
and America. It sent shivers down the spines of
Londoners and for a long time limited the activi-
ties of the class among whom the maniac selected
his victims. The authorities being unable to
obtain a single clue, numerous private citizens
enlisted as detectives. Even one of the autocratic
directors of the Bank of London disguised himself
as a laborer and in heavy boots and fustian jacket,
with a red bandanna tied about his head and a
pickax over his shoulder, sought diversion each
night haunting neighborhoods in which he imag-
ined "Jack the Ripper" would appear.

The distinguished criminologist, L. Forbes

Winslow, spent night after night in the Whitechapel slums seeking the slayer and at one time
inserted in the London papers an advertisement
stating that a gentleman strongly opposed to the
presence of fallen women in the streets of London
would like to co-operate in their suppression. By
this means Doctor Winslow hoped to get into
correspondence with the maniac, and he received
several confessions in the same handwriting. Each
expressed insane glee over the hideous work, and
one stated that the next murder would be committed on November 9th. The fact that this
prophecy was brutally fulfilled led the doctor to
believe that he had been in correspondence with
"Jack the Ripper" himself, although previously
he had suspected that some one was hoaxing him.
On the day prophesied the body of Mary Anne
Kelly, with throat cut and body eviscerated, was
found on a ground-floor room with an uncurtained
window through which any passerby might have
seen the crime, which had been committed in
broad daylight.   In the handwriting of Doctor
Winslow's correspondent was at last found beneath
an archway the statement: "Jack the Ripper will
never commit another murder."   And this prophecy also seems to have been fulfilled.

Every investigator of the crimes had his own
theory as to "Jack the Ripper's" character.

He was variously believed to be an escaped gorilla, a Russian discharged from a Paris asylum; a man from Vienna, who, in a London Hospital, had complained of having been robbed by a street-walker, and who after threatening to kill all such women, had exhibited surgical interest by asking to witness various operations; and a sufferer from masked epilepsy, who during his chronic seizures would perform the most diabolical acts, but who on returning to consciousness was in entire ignorance of his crimes.

Because a slaughter house was found to be in close proximity to each spot in which a victim was found, one investigator, applying the law of deduction, argued that "Jack the Ripper" was a butcher, and on the strength of this theory several detectives disguised as slaughtermen went to work in these establishments. One theory was that the murderer was a woman disguised as a slaughterman.

The belief of Doctor Winslow is that "Jack the Ripper" was a man of position and means—a Doctor Jekyll and Mr. Hyde phenomenon suffering from a religious monomania, and who, while his paroxysms lasted, was bent on exterminating fallen women, but who, when these seizures passed off, returned to the bosom of his family, probably in the West End of London.

The favorite theory has been that "Jack the Ripper" practiced his butchery in revenge for having contracted from a woman of Whitechapel an incurable disease which had undermined his health and unhinged his reason.

Who he was and why he plied his hideous trade is the sphinx riddle of criminology.

The Borden Murder Mystery

Of American murder mysteries the Borden case, at Fall River, Mass., in the late summer of 1892, was doubtless the most notorious. On the morning of August 4th Mr. and Mrs. Andrew J. Borden, wealthy residents of that city, were found murdered in their home, Mrs. Borden in a guest chamber upstairs and Mr. Borden in a room upon the ground floor. The only other known occupants of the house at the time were Bridget Sullivan, a maid of all work, and Lizzie Borden, the unmarried daughter of the murdered man by his first wife.

Andrew Borden was seventy and his wife six years his junior. Although he was alleged to be worth $300,000, they lived with the modest thrift of the New England family of the middle class. Lizzie Borden was thirty-two. She had an elder sister who, at the time of the tragedy, was away on a visit.

Two days before the murder Mr. and Mrs. Borden were taken suddenly ill with violent nausea, Lizzie Borden being also slightly affected. The next day Miss Lizzie complained to a neighbor that men with whom her father had had trouble were evidently trying to poison the family. This was Wednesday.

On Thursday morning, that of the murder, Bridget Sullivan also suffered nausea just after breakfast. Recovering, she found Mrs. Borden dusting the parlor, whereupon the old lady, after directing the servant to wash the windows, had started for the second floor to arrange the guest room. This, about 9.30 A. M., was the last time Mrs. Borden was seen alive.

Lizzie Borden was in the kitchen when Bridget started to wash the windows. Mr. Borden soon afterward came in from town, and, finding the back screen door hooked, was let in by Bridget at the front door, which was locked. At 10.45 Lizzie entered the parlor and told her father that Mrs. Borden had gotten a note from some sick person and had gone out. Mr. Borden then went up the back stairs to his room, which he kept locked, and which did not communicate with the front part of the second floor, which contained the guest room.

At this point Bridget commenced on the

windows in the dining-room, where Lizzie was now ironing. The latter repeated to Bridget that Mrs. Borden had been called out by a note and in a quarter hour Bridget went up to her room, above Mr. Borden's. Ten minutes later the servant heard Miss Borden shriek that her father had been murdered downstairs.

Bridget, after being sent for the doctor and while the neighbors came pouring in, proposed to go about town and look for Mrs. Borden, but Lizzie stated that she thought she had heard the old lady return. The servant and a neighbor then went upstairs and found Mrs. Borden murdered on the floor of the guest room, whose door was open. When asked where she was just before discovering the murder, Miss Borden claimed that she was at the barn, but made conflicting statements as to what she was doing there. Although many thought these were due to nervous confusion, she was arrested and tried for the crime.

It was unfortunate for Lizzie Borden that she and her stepmother had not agreed, and that she and her father had fallen out over the transfer of some property to the second wife. But it was shown that this sore had been partially healed by the old man's making financial compensation to his daughters. Another fact used against Miss Borden was that some days after the murder she had burned a dress, saying that it was full of paint, but it was shown that she did this openly, in the presence of a neighbor, and that it was the family custom to burn old clothes. It was furthermore contended by the prosecutor that, save during Mr. Borden's entrance, the front door had been locked during the whole morning of the crime and the night before, and that the murderer of Mrs. Borden could have entered only through the kitchen door and have reached the victims only by traversing the rooms whose windows the servant was washing most of the time.

Altogether twenty-nine wounds, evidently from a sharp hatchet, were found on the two old people, and the rooms in which they were found were badly splattered with blood. What freed Lizzie Borden was the fact that no suspicious weapon or implement was discovered in the house and no blood stains were upon her clothes.

The medical testimony showed that the step-mother had been killed before Lizzie had talked with Bridget, during the ironing, and that the father had died subsequent to this conversation. So to have killed the two old people Miss Borden would have had to make at least two changes of clothes, the last one within ten minutes after the killing. Within this same time she would also have had to dispose of the weapon used.

She was acquitted on the first ballot.

A farmer of the neighborhood stated that while in his woods after the crime he had heard a weird voice repeat three times, "Poor Mrs. Borden," and had thereupon come upon a man, with blood spots on his shirt, who took up a hatchet and shook it at him. The farmer then raised his ax in an attitude of defense and the mysterious stranger, leaping over a wall, had disappeared into the black depths of the wood.

In our criminal annals there has never been a trial that has left both participants and onlookers in such deep perplexity, and has divided them into so many factions, each holding stubbornly to a definite theory.

The Maybrick Case

"One man's poison is another man's meat. There is a so-called poison which is meat and liquor to me whenever I feel weak and depressed. I don't tell everybody and wouldn't tell you, only you mentioned arsenic. It is arsenic."

Had this confession of an arsenic-eater been related at the proper time, fate might have dealt differently with an American woman who was the chief actor in one of the most perplexing mysteries of modern times.

Mary Elizabeth Chandler was the daughter of

a prosperous banker of Mobile, Ala. Her father
died when she was a year old, and after her
mother's marriage to the Baron von Roques she
divided her time between Europe and America.
At the age of eighteen, when a wholesome,
vivacious girl, fond of outdoor sports, she married
James Maybrick, of Liverpool, near which city
the couple made their home. During the second
year of their marriage a son was born to them
and, later, a daughter.

Maybrick was twenty-seven years the senior
of his wife. For eight years their married life
was happy and contented. Then, of a sudden,
they quarreled, Maybrick losing his temper so far
as to blacken his wife's eye and attempt to turn
her into the streets. The discovery of mutual
intrigues is said to have been the cause of this
infelicity. The young wife initiated divorce pro-
ceedings, but for the sake of the children became
apparently reconciled to her husband. A few
weeks later, in the spring of 1889, Maybrick was
taken ill, and after several days he died. The
family physician had treated him for dyspepsia,
although it was constantly suggested by the
patient's brother, Michael Maybrick, that poison
was the cause of his illness. The discovery of
more than seventy grains of arsenic in the house
after the death led to an autopsy, which, however,

revealed no arsenic in the stomach or any weigh-
able traces of the poison in any other parts of the
body.   But as a result of insistence by the Maybrick family, the body was exhumed three weeks
later and about one-tenth of a grain of arsenic was
found in the viscera.   Although the smallest fatal
dose of the drug on record is known to be two
grains, the widow of the dead man was arrested
and imprisoned.

Her trial was a long one, and the family physicians swore that but for the discovery of arsenic
on the premises they would have given a certificate
of death from natural causes.   The defendant's
counsel proved that for twenty years Maybrick
had been a confirmed arsenic-eater and that he
daily took doses that would have killed a dozen
ordinary men.   A Liverpool druggist testified
that the dead man had lately been in the habit
of calling several times a day at his shop to get
doses of a proprietary tonic to which he had
added a large proportion of arsenic.   One of the
family doctors gave evidence that during the
year prior to Maybrick's death his wife had
appealed to him to influence her husband against
the habitual use of certain tonics and white
powders which she believed to be doing him
harm.   It was the contention of the defendant's
counsel that the minute quantity of arsenic found

in the body was readily accounted for by Maybrick's habits as an arsenic-eater.

But a circumstance brought out by the prosecution weighed against the defendant. This was the fact that she had bought flypaper containing arsenic which she had soaked out, confessedly for use as a face bleach.

Yet if, as charged, she had previously purchased the seventy grains already on hand in the house, why should she have openly manufactured more arsenic by soaking flypaper? Moreover, Mrs. Maybrick's innocence was indicated by the fact that she had been the first to give the alarm of her husband's illness, to send for his doctors, brothers and friends and to suggest that some drug was at the bottom of his illness. Before the physician's arrival she had administered to him a mustard emetic, which she would not have done had she desired the poison to take effect. Her lawyer stated that "if she had wished to put everybody in the house and the doctors themselves on the scent of poison, she could not have acted differently."

Sir Fitzjames Stephen, the presiding judge for two days, delivered to the jury a charge which in the beginning favored the prisoner, but which toward the end showed bias against her, and as a result the jury brought in a verdict of guilty,

18

after being out only thirty-eight minutes. Shortly afterward the judge wrote that out of nine hundred and seventy-nine suits tried before him that of Mrs. Maybrick "was the only case in which there could be any doubt about the facts." After the trial her case threw him into a morbid state of brooding, which developed into madness from which he never recovered. The Liverpool *Post*, previously hostile to Mrs. Maybrick, now recalled the famous trial in these words:

"In fancy one still hears the distant fanfare of the trumpets as the judges with quaint pageantry pass down the hall, and still the mind's eye sees the crimson-clad figure of the great mad judge as he sat down to try his last case. A tragedy indeed was played upon the bench no less than in the dock."

Justice Stephen sentenced Mrs. Maybrick to be hanged. After she had languished in the shadow of the scaffold for several weeks (the English law forbidding her to know when the execution was to come) she was at last warned to prepare for death. But almost at the last moment her sentence was commuted to life imprisonment.

After she had been imprisoned for eleven years, it was discovered that Lord Russell, Chief Justice of England, had before his death written to her a letter in which he said:

"I feel as strongly as I have felt from the first that you should never have been convicted, and this opinion I have very clearly expressed to Mr. Asquith, but, I am sorry to say, hitherto without effect."

By persistent diplomatic overtures, our government pleaded for Mrs. Maybrick's pardon, but not until she had languished in prison for fifteen years was she finally released on "ticket of leave."

The confession quoted at the head of this article was made by Maybrick to Valentine Blake. son of a British knight and member of Parliament, but did not come to light until after Mrs. Maybrick's trial.